THE
BLUES
ROUTE

Hugh Merrill

WILLIAM MORROW AND COMPANY, INC.
NEW YORK

Library of Congress Cataloging-in-Publication Data

Merrill, Hugh.
   The blues route / Hugh Merrill.
     p. cm.
   ISBN 0-688-06611-9
   1. Blues (Music)—History and criticism. I. Title.
ML3521.M47   1990
781.643'097309048—dc20   90-30754
                                                CIP

Printed in the United States of America

First Edition

1 2 3 4 5 6 7 8 9 10

BOOK DESIGN BY M.C. DEMAIO DESIGNS

For Jacinta

ACKNOWLEDGMENTS

A LOT OF PEOPLE were helpful along the Blues Route, and without their offers of food, shelter, and general encouragement this book might not have been possible. I particularly want to thank Worth Long, Bruce Iglauer, Carol and Stonewall Stickney, Ben Sandmill, Richard and Yvonne Williams, Sue and Barry Corbin, Jim Stafford, Crista Sides, Jack and Betty Miller, Donna and Ernie Ellingson, Ronnie Dugger, Bob and Mary Sherrill, Mike and Marlene Zeiler, Jim and Carol O'Kon, Jay Acton, Inge Hanson, Jim Landis, Doug Stumpf, and Jared Stamm.

Most of all, though, I would like to thank my wife, Ja. She offered ideas, suggestions, criticism and, most of all, the support and belief I needed to finish this project. No written words can thank her enough. I love her.

INTRODUCTION

BLUES HARBOR IS A nightclub in Atlanta's Buckhead district, a glittering cornpone Beverly Hills on the north side of town. It's about a mile away from Neiman-Marcus and Lord & Taylor and even closer to the Texas State Line Barbecue where a plate of ribs costs twelve dollars.

In the 1920s, Barbecue Bob and Charlie Lincoln worked in Buckhead at another more reasonably priced barbecue stand that served Georgia pork rather than smoked Texas beef. When they weren't cleaning windshields and serving barbecue, they played and recorded the blues.

Back then, Buckhead was a remote outpost, twelve miles away from Decatur Street in downtown Atlanta, where Bessie Smith performed inside Bailey's 81 Theater and Peg Leg Howell played outside, hustling tips from the crowd waiting to get in. But the blues didn't stay in Atlanta long. Barbecue Bob died drunk when he was twenty-nine, Charlie Lincoln went to jail for murder and died in prison, and the old 81 Theater on Decatur Street was demolished.

The blues went underground, surfacing occasionally on Auburn Avenue at such clubs as the Royal Peacock, but for the most part vanishing under the increasing commercial pressures of rock and roll and soul music. Now it has come back to Atlanta, or more properly to Buckhead, nestled between glittering discotheques and fashionable boutiques.

I grew up in Anniston, Alabama, and the blues was as much a part of my life as spoonbread and turnip greens. Clara Fuller sang them in my kitchen at breakfast. An old blind man sat in a ladderback chair on the corner of Tenth and Noble Streets and played slide guitar for tips, as lawyers walked by on their way to the courthouse. Around the corner, near the Wilson Building, a fruit peddler called The Banana Man advertised his specials in a bluesy chant. As a child I heard the yardmen and domestics singing the blues in nearby backyards. As a teenager I hung around the two-bit studios of a radio station that specialized in the blues every afternoon. At night I would ride slowly past the mysterious Blue Light Savoy in West Anniston and hear the music drifting out on blue clouds of tobacco smoke.

The blues was never a rich-man's music, even after Hollywood and Broadway got hold of it. So it seemed strange that Atlanta's new blues joint would be in a neighborhood of ostentatious wealth. It seemed even stranger that Blues Harbor offered lobster-and-steak dinners and was decorated with chandeliers, a padded bar, waitresses and waiters in Oxford-cloth shirts and wide, red suspenders.

Against one wall there is a raised, wooden platform where real blues aficionados, uninterested in lobster dinners, can drink a beer and listen to music. It's like sitting in the bleachers of a small high school gymnasium. The show starts at ten. I arrive at eight to get a good seat. The room is filling with people dressed as if they were attending a charity benefit. Occasionally, a woman comes in who has decided to slum it in a pink velvet jogging suit and a strand of opera-length pearls. The recorded background music is Glenn Miller. Everyone is white. On my right a man talks to his date with passion about the advantages of a gold American Express Card. On my left, a blonde pulls her head out of a table lantern she is using to light her cigarette and talks about the music she will be hearing later. "They say this is the Chicago blues. Well, I hope it's better than what they've got to offer in the Chicago art museums. When I went up there, they had a picture of a leaf. Just a regular leaf and it cost two hundred dollars. It wasn't even in pretty fall colors. Can you imagine that?"

After a while, the band, most of them in their fifties or sixties, comes in and walks past the patrons to the back. Outside the rest rooms is a padded bench. That's their dressing room and their lounge between sets.

"Oh," says the blonde as she puffs on her cigarette, "are those the boys we're gonna hear tonight?"

A half hour later the band is onstage playing steamy, Chicago blues. No one is paying attention. The audience treats the musicians as live background music. The band members look at each other and shrug. They begin to vamp. The audience doesn't notice. Finally, in desperation, the band starts singing dirty songs filled with double entendres. A few drunks laugh at the nasty lyrics, but the room is still filled with the buzz of conversation. After a forty-five-minute set, the band retreats to its bench for a twenty-minute break.

My God, I thought, *is this what the blues has come to? Where's the electricity? Where's the emotion?* I remembered what one woman from Louisiana once told me: "On Saturday night, we all let our hair get a little bit kinky."

I paid for my beer and left. Surely this is not all there was. On my way home, I decided that I would find out. The greatest migration in America took the blues as baggage—from the Mississippi Delta to Chicago and from

INTRODUCTION

Louisiana and Texas to California. I decided to re-create the trip. I imagined myself in an old blue Cadillac, fish-tailing it down Highway 61 with a tape recorder in the backseat, waiting to discover American music that had never been heard before. But I realized those days were gone, too. Folklorists and record executives had already mined those fields. Still, I could not get the idea out of my mind.

What happened to the blues in the decades after the civil-rights movement? Was that music nothing more than a memory? I knew I couldn't make the trip in an old Cadillac. My Honda would have to do. I went home, packed my clothes, and got out a map. Tomorrow I would leave the memories of Blues Harbor behind me and set out on The Blues Route.

1

IT'S A LONG, uneventful drive from Atlanta to Mississippi. The highway winds past the rusting steel mills in the Appalachian foothills near Birmingham, then flattens out after Tuscaloosa for a straight shot to Jackson, interrupted only by an interchange at Meridian and an occasional billboard. There's not much to do but watch the road and twist the radio dial.

I drive past Villa Rica and Temple, Georgia. The early blues have become synonymous with the Mississippi Delta, but in 1915, Ma Rainey of Columbus, Georgia, "The Golden Necklace of the Blues," was singing in a tent show called *Fat Chappelle's Rabbit Foot Minstrels*. Her warm-up act was a Chattanooga street singer named Bessie Smith. Maybe I should stay in Georgia. Then, as I cross the state line, I remember a Florence, Alabama, composer named William Christopher Handy. After moving to Memphis and writing songs about Boss Crump, Beale Street, St. James Infirmary, and St. Louis, he became known as "The Father of the Blues." Maybe I should turn north.

As I drive through Pell City and Leeds, I remember something I read in Handy's biography years before. He wrote about waiting on a train one night in 1903 at Tutwiler, Mississippi, in the heart of the Delta. The train was nine hours late, and as Handy dozed, he was awakened by a black man playing a guitar and rubbing the blade of his knife against the strings. It made a sound Handy thought was "weird." He opened his eyes and heard the man sing about going "where the Southern crosses the Yellow Dog." "What," Handy asked, "does that mean?" The singer explained that he was from Moorehead, where the Yazoo and Mississippi Railroad, known as "The Yellow Dog," crossed the tracks of the Southern Railroad. He was singing about going home. Eight years later, Handy published his first blues, based on what he heard that lonesome Mississippi night. I push down on the accelerator. I haven't made a mistake. I need to go to the Delta.

Of course the blues means different things to different people. To some it's early New Orleans jazz, to others it's after-hours music played in a smoky jazz club at three in the morning, or the Kansas City jazz of Count Basie or Jay McShann; to still others it's the plaintive and sometimes mysterious guitar and singing of such Delta bluesmen as Robert Johnson, or the barrelhouse piano of William Bunch, aka Peetie Wheatstraw, aka The Devil's Son-in-Law, aka The High Sheriff from Hell. There are people who associate blues with such vaudeville singers as Ma Rainey, Ida Cox, or Bessie Smith, who played in the *Silas Green*, from New Orleans, or *Rabbit Foot*, minstrels shows; or with such Chicago musicians as Muddy Waters or Howlin' Wolf. In a way, they're all right.

> *The Concise Oxford Dictionary of Music* says the blues is: . . . a sort of bitter-sweet jazz song or dance song written in quadruple time, generally moving at slow speed and in more or less flowing style over an unvarying 12-bar bass. Stanzas are of three lines, each covering four bars of music.

The third and seventh of the key are often prominent, being played somewhere between the major and minor form of the interval and are known as blue notes.

Yeah, well. The standard definitions of the blues would make you think the music, always said to have come up with black people through slavery and misery, is nothing but a mournful dirge. As Ma Rainey sang, "Take me to the basement, that's as low as I can go." Sometimes, of course, the music is sad. But there's another side to the blues that's never taken into account in the dictionary definitions. The blues can drive away your troubles, not just reinforce them. It can produce emotional catharsis with frenzied dance music. As Albert Murray wrote in *Stomping the Blues*:

> The irrepressible joyousness, the downright exhilaration, the rapturous delight in sheer physical existence, like the elegant jocularity and hearty nonsense that are no less characteristic of blues music, are unsurpassed by any other dance music in the world. Still, the captivating elegance that always seems so entirely innate to blues idiom dance movement is something earned in a context of antagonism. It has been achieved through the manifestation of grace under pressure. . . . As to the matter of dispersing gloom and spreading glee, evidence in favor of the sorcery of Madam Marie Laveau, also known as the Widow Paris, the most notorious New Orleans voodoo queen, and the mojo hands of Dr. Jim Alexander, né Charles La Fountain, also known as Indian Jim, her male

counterpart, is questionable to say the least. Testimony that the dance-beat incantation and percussion of Bessie Smith and Louis Armstrong almost always worked as advertised is universal.

Or, more simply, as the Living Queen of the Blues, Koko Taylor, sings:

Tell Automatic Slim,
Tell Razor Totin' Jim,
Tell Butcher Knife Totin' Annie,
Tell Fast Talkin' Fannie.
We gonna pitch a ball
Down to that Union Hall.
We gonna romp and stomp till midnight.
We gonna fuss and fight till daylight.
When the fish scent fills the air,
There'll be snuff juice everywhere.
We gonna pitch a Wang Dang Doodle all night long.

I hit Jackson by sundown—not quite the Delta, but at least the home of Malaco Records, a money-making blues label run by two white boys who graduated from Ole Miss. It seems a logical place to start.

The next morning I drive out to the north edge of town to talk to Stewart Madison, president of Malaco. He is in his office, down a twisting corridor and through a couple of doors, past a room where the muffled sound of electric guitar and drums can be heard through heavy burlap padding. The insistent thump of the music carries into Madison's office, and as we talk, the muffled drum punctuates our conversation.

Stewart Madison says, despite what anybody else tells

you, Malaco is not a blues label. Blues doesn't make money. Rhythm and blues—the rock and roll of the late fifties— does. And Malaco, he says, is in business to make money. "We don't cut blues here," he says as he sits behind a desk littered with racing forms, records, and contracts. "With straight blues you have a limited audience, and it ain't gonna grow. Once in a while, we'll drop back and cut a couple of low-downs, but we make records for black people. And the black audience for real deep blues is not big."

Madison is talking about the blues, but his mind is on the Keeneland thoroughbred sales in Lexington, Kentucky. He interrupts our conversation to take a phone call and make a bid on a horse. "I own about five thoroughbreds," he says after he hangs up, "but, first of all, I'm a gambler. I'll always go to the races—dogs, horses, you name it, I'll be there. I can understand any racing form that's ever come out."

What about Little Milton? I ask him, steering the conversation back to music, or Z. Z. Hill?—two musicians who record for Malaco. Aren't they singing the blues? I mean, people talk about the blues today and they talk about Z. Z. Hill's record of "Down Home Blues" or Little Milton's version of "The Blues Is All Right."

"Well, of course they're gonna categorize Z. Z. Hill as a blues artist, but he also recorded rhythm and blues. And that makes him more than just a blues singer," Madison says. "Now, Little Milton is closer to a blues artist but the album he has out now—it's sold about fifty thousand copies—is not a blues album either. I really don't know these blues people. If we encouraged this type of artist we'd have 'em up and down the aisles, but there's just not enough volume in it to get us interested. It's as hard to get blues played on a black radio station as it is to get bluegrass played on a country station," Madison says. "They play it, oh, maybe once a week when they take you way back. Like bluegrass and opera, deep blues is fringe music. You have a certain audience that's gonna buy anything that comes out, but that audience is very, very small. And it's not gonna grow. Now you take that fellow you hear in there. His name is George Jackson and he wrote "Down Home Blues" and "Cheatin' in the Next Room" and he also wrote "Old Time Rock and Roll" recorded by Bob Seger. These guys cross over. Blues has a limited audience, man, and it just ain't gonna grow. Rhythm and blues is what Malaco does."

Truthfully, Malaco records sound less like blues and more like a latter-day version of Stax, the Memphis record company that produced albums by Rufus Thomas, Isaac Hayes and Booker T. and the MGs. Stax, along with Motown in Detroit, was the genesis of soul music. It's no wonder Malaco has adapted that sound. Madison's partner, Tommy Couch, who produces most of Malaco's records, is from Tuscumbia, a west Alabama town near Muscle Shoals that's only about a hundred miles from Memphis. There was a brief flurry of musical activity in Muscle Shoals during the sixties when Ahmet Ertegun of Atlantic Records sent people down there to record, but it's mostly faded now. "All those guys in Muscle Shoals were my friends, and that's how I got in the business," Couch says. "They started out doing black music but they're in Nashville now, doing country."

Then he returned to his ideas about the blues.

"You know, the audience for the blues—I would think it would be very eccentric people who think it's 'in' right now. There are very few stone-blues lovers out there who love to hear the raw thing. Now, blues do very well in the

East. I think they get a lot of sales because the records go to specialty shops and make it available to the white community. But all the people I talk to all day are selling black records to black people. There's just not enough volume in the blues to get us interested. We're a little record company and we're fighting for record sales to survive. Most everything we put out has got to sell fifty thousand or above. But the thing is, if you and I were sitting at CBS and you played the president of that company my product, he'd say it's not commercial. See, they have to sell about a hundred thousand albums to make it worthwhile. We got to sell about twenty thousand.

"The difference between Bruce Iglauer with Alligator Records in Chicago and Malaco is that he's really into what he's doing in the sense that he gets too involved with his artists. We put out records sometimes that are not our favorite records, but we're putting out what's good of its kind. I probably wouldn't play it in my car all day, but I understand there is some demand. We're starting to put out some beat records, street records. There ain't no musicians at all on them. We don't cut those records here, we license them from other producers. You know, all it is, is two machines and a guy.

"Let's face it, blues is a lot like opera. You have a certain audience that's gonna buy almost anything of that, but it's a very small group of people.

"You take Mississippi Fred McDowell. We used to have him on Malaco and all these blues people you're talking about loved Fred McDowell. Everywhere we would go there would be this group of people, a very small group but a loyal group. They'd be in almost every urban area. So, Fred thought everybody all over the world was like that. He thought there were masses of people who loved him. But there were just a handful of liberal whites. For a liberal white it was sort of fashionable to like that. But for the masses, they just go for the popular stuff.

"We recorded Fred in 1969 and I think he died in 1970. He was just a nice guy, an old guy, an old black gentleman. His world was really kinda small other than every year or two when he went on tour. You know, he even played with The Beatles. But at the same time, he'd get real impressed when he came to Jackson. He was from Como, Mississippi, and he'd worked in Stuckey's up there for years and years. He had a good understanding about everything. He would talk about how to make sure he got a tip at Stuckey's, about how to always clean the windshield when a car drove up. He'd even clean the headlight. He was smart. We'd be in the studio and we'd record a song and he'd mess up and we'd have to do it again. And every time he'd change the lyrics. It would be a different song, basically the same but a verse here and there different. He didn't know any better. He didn't care. There are a few old guys left playing the blues, but it's probably gonna be all over in the next few years when these guys die. The young people who are playing the blues are mostly white, because the young black musicians see how much Michael Jackson is making."

Mississippi may be the home of the blues, but at Malaco the native music isn't profitable. Maybe that's why they put the music in a museum in Clarksdale, a few hours up the Delta from Jackson. I planned to spend some time there after I stopped for the annual blues festival at Greenville.

Originally, I intended to drive from Jackson to Greenville on the fabled Highway 61, but a secretary at Malaco persuaded me to change my route. "Go up Highway Forty-nine," she says, "It's scenic. You can see 'em harvesting the catfish and the cotton is open." Ira Gershwin said the same thing over fifty years before in *Porgy and Bess*: "Fish are jumpin' and the cotton is high." Who could resist it? As I check out of the Holiday Inn to travel down Highway 49 through Yazoo City and on to Greenville, the black bellman drops the copy of *Blues Who's Who*, by Sheldon Harris, which I carry everywhere. As he picks it up and puts it on the backseat he says; "You know, I hear people say that every black man has the blues. And it's like a cancer. It'll eat you alive if you don't let it out."

"Do you believe that?" I ask him.

"Oh, hell no," he answers.

In its vastness and silence, there is something awesome, even eerie about the Mississippi Delta. It may be the only part of the region where Atlanta journalist Henry Grady's talk of a "New South" fell on deaf ears. By the side of the road and back across the enormous expanse of cotton, there are small row houses that look no different from the black-and-white pictures Walker Evans shot in the midst of the Depression. Small towns like Louise, Midnight, and Anguilla—tiny crossroads settlements with a general store, a gas station, and a post office. But there is one difference. In the days of Walker Evans the small cafés that dotted the side of the road were unpainted shacks called juke joints where you could hear the blues every night. They are still there, but now the small buildings are brightly painted and called discos. There are few columned antebellum houses of the type mythically associated with the cotton South. The northern Delta was little more than a snarled expanse of canebrakes and forests during the Civil War. Cleveland, a Delta town of thirteen thousand, is not even a hundred years old.

While the blues were everywhere in the cotton South—in Alabama, Georgia, Louisiana, and Texas as well as in this rich agricultural area—the Delta is the place the blues is said to have been born.

The roots of blues are the rhythms of Africa. In Africa, long before the first black man came to America, music involved drumming, call-and-response group singing, hand clapping, falsetto singing, and moaning. But the blues is not African music. Samuel Charters went to Africa to find the origins of the blues. And while he found some music that was similar, he came to the conclusion in *The Roots of the Blues, An African Search*: "Things in the blues had come from the tribal musicians of the old kingdoms, but as a style the blues represented something else. It was essentially a new kind of song that had begun with the new life in the American South."

The first real antecedents of the blues came from days of slavery—the field holler, work songs involving call-and-response patterns, the black string bands that formed on plantations to entertain the whites in the Big House. And, of course, there's the influence of the church and early spirituals—often standard hymns transformed when they encountered an African tradition.

But it took freedom to birth the blues. After the Civil War, black musicians were free to travel, develop their repertoire, and combine their traditions with those from other areas. They could also use drums, something that had been forbidden on most plantations. These traveling musicians were called songsters, musicianers, or physician-ers. They played black versions of minstrel songs and white country-music ballads. By the turn of the century, a distinctive black form called the jump-up had developed. And the jump-up begot the blues as surely as the blues begot jazz and rock and roll.

In Alabama and Georgia, the blues tradition was more melodic with a heavier emphasis on ballad structure and the faint beginnings of the boogie-woogie. In Texas and Oklahoma the blues started to swing, giving birth to groups as diverse as the Count Basie Band and Bob Wills and the Texas Playboys. In Mississippi there was a raw sound that would spawn such musicians as Charley Patton, the first recorded blues singer, Son House, Robert Johnson, and, ultimately, Muddy Waters, Howlin' Wolf, and even Elvis Presley.

Somewhere near Louise, I stop at what looks like a double-wide mobile home with a couple of gas pumps out front and a dented Coca-Cola sign on the roof. Inside, a middle-aged man with a face the color of lightly tanned leather sits and looks out the window. Behind him is a woman of indeterminate age, who sits in a wheelchair and stares stoically at a small television.

"What part of Georgia you from?" the man asks.

"Atlanta," I say as I pay for my gasoline.

"I just come back from Georgia," he says. "I was an ironworker. Worked down near Savannah. Been doing it maybe forty year. But my baby here," he nods at the woman in the wheelchair, "it was hard on her, living in hotels and all. So we were over here visitin' and I told somebody that me and Baby was tired of traveling and if this store was for sale, I'd buy it. Well, it was, and I did. That was about two months ago. I guess we're settled now, ain't we, Baby?"

Baby smiles in silence at the television.

"What you doing over here?" he asks.

"Looking for the blues," I answer.

"Oh, you'll find 'em. No question about that. You'll find the blues in the Delta." He watches me as I drive off toward Greenville.

There should be no problem finding the blues this weekend. The seventh annual Delta Blues Festival is scheduled to take place in the middle of a cotton field in a new community near Greenville called Freedom Village. Unlike most festivals, this one is sponsored by a black community group. They're interested in the traditions born in Mississippi, but they have to make certain concessions to commercialism. Early Saturday morning, the crowd begins to gather. The salt-and-pepper crowd, heavy on the pepper, swells from about five thousand, when the festival opens with the primitive strains of the Mississippi Fife and Drum band, to thirty thousand by the time Albert King finishes playing around midnight. For the first time, the T-shirts and posters advertise the DELTA BLUES—RHYTHM AND BLUES FESTIVAL.

Bo Diddley, one of the headliners, shows up early. He's not scheduled to play until that night, so he spends most of the afternoon being photographed in his size-fifty-nine Italian police hat, doing a modified cancan with blond co-eds and giving interviews. Once, years ago, Bo Diddley the gunslinger was bad. The thrill an Ole Miss white coed would have had rubbing up against him would have been akin to driving ninety miles an hour down a dead-end street. But he is older now and safe. So the sorority girls give him chaste pecks on the cheek and press discreetly against him when pictures are taken.

A lot of television cameras and radio microphones

move in on Bo and Mrs. Diddley, so he holds an impromptu news conference:

"The rich man, the richest mother on earth has got the blues every day when he goes to bed at night. He's got the blues. When he wakes up in the morning, he's got the blues. And he's got all the money, ya dig it? 'Cause he's trying to think about how to keep you from getting it. A lot of the younger generation is trying to interpret blues as what they think it is without going to the roots," Bo Diddley says, "without finding out from the older cats, you know, without finding out what inspired them to do down-home country blues. I've had cats tell me, 'Say, hey, man, that tune you do called "Who Do You Love," that's a blues number.' That's not blues. That's what I call a comical rhythm-and-blues song. It's not just plain blues. Now, I don't play the blues. I play rhythm and blues. And there's a difference. The source for me is that I created my own sound. I didn't have to have a source because I don't play blues. I didn't copy after anybody because I don't sound like nobody else. They all try to sound like me. The current black musicians like Michael Jackson, they don't have no direction.

"You listen to the radio right now and you don't hear much blues or rhythm and blues because you don't have a lot of black kids who's interested. They've been poisoned with this other bullshit. And it's ruining a lot of potentially good musicians. OK, it's making money. But how can this go down in the history book of music if it's done so shabby? They gonna wake up and realize that the stuff they're playing is not gonna be standard tunes. You know with a lot of that stuff you can't jump back and say, 'Oh! That was a legendary tune.' Now tunes like, 'Bo Diddley' and 'I'm a Man' is in the history books. The best songs, they tell a story. A sucker gets up on the stage and hollers, 'Yeah, yeah, yeah' for twenty minutes and then at the end of it he hollers 'I do.' To me that ain't nothing. We got problems in this business. And nobody knows which way to go. OK, you got the disco that's trying to hang on and you got rhythm and blues that's trying to stay in there and you got what they call rock—which ain't rock and roll—and they're all trying to find a slot. It's a rat race. Nobody has any identity. It's the record companies that are doing it. You turn on your radio right now and you'll hear the deejay say, 'OK, we're gonna get back to some good old rock and roll.' Shit. Call it new music, call it anything you want to. But it ain't rock and roll. I call it leak over from the acid-rock days."

As the reporters drift away, he sits on the fender of a pickup truck and talks in hushed tones to Mrs. Diddley.

I could argue, I guess, about whether Lynn White from Mobile sings the blues or not—she certainly sounds bluesy enough, and she's the sexiest woman I've seen on stage since Tina Turner was in her thirties. Her music is earthy and she bumps and grinds to the heavy beat, with a red dress molded to her body. The dress is slit up the sides and her long legs peek out, just like a stripper's. The audience loves it, and so do I, but from time to time it begins to sound like soul music.

Out in front of the stage, the crowd mills about sampling the barbecued ribs for sale, buys T-shirts with the festival logo painted on them, or walks to the smaller stages that feature a blues alternative to the big acts up front. There are long lines at the portable toilets, a testament to the volume of beer sales. The festival has a country, down-home flavor to it. I listen and mill for a few hours but then the music develops a sameness about it. It's like whiskey.

After the second or third drink, it's hard to tell rotgut from Jack Daniels. I decide to leave Freedom Village and go down to Nelson Street.

Blues historians made Nelson Street famous, and Willie Love honored it in a song called "Nelson Street Blues." For years, musicians from up and down the Delta went to this shabby block of disheveled juke joints to play on Saturday night. Every black man with a guitar or harmonica, famous or unknown, claims to have been there at least once. Jim O'Neal, editor of *Living Blues*, told me he was hustled in a Nelson Street bar by a two-hundred-pound black woman truck driver. Nelson Street is not a country club.

It does, however, have a Playboy Club, a former used-furniture store emblazoned with spray-painted rabbit heads on the wall. The Playboy Club is not part of the now-defunct Hefner chain and there are no bunnies inside; it is the home of Booby Barnes. His family lives in the back, often oblivious to the raucous weekend behavior in the area that once displayed sofas, chairs, and box springs and mattresses. Women have been thrown out of the bar for performing what one writer delicately called, "bedroom maneuvers" on the dance floor or stripping to beat the heat. On Saturday nights, the party continues until five in the morning, with the clanking of beer bottles acting as percussion for Booby's blues band. From time to time, Barnes's children walk in sleepily from their bedroom in the back, presumably in search of a parent or a glass of water.

I wandered up the street past other bars and lounges and eventually ended up in Nelson Street's one white joint, Doe's Eat Place. It's a shotgun house near the levee that opened as a grocery store for the black community in 1903.

Doe's Grocery Store was owned by the Italian parents of Dominic "Doe" Signa. Times got hard during the Depression, and Doe had to hustle for money. He turned the front room of the store into a honky-tonk specializing in hot tamales to accompany the bootleg liquor he served to his black customers. By the end of World War II, the joint's reputation had spread to the white gentry of Greenville and they began to sneak into the back room for a libation and a tamale or two. After broiled steaks were added to the menu a few years later, black customers were barred. Any man with skin darker than a brown paper bag wasn't allowed in Doe's until after the 1964 Civil Rights Act was passed.

The night I was there, the back room was filled with a bunch of Ole Miss graduates. They talked mostly about football, and occasionally expressed bewilderment that so many people would show up in town to hear the blues. Doe's looks like a run-down country store, but it is famous for steaks, not decor. The slabs of beef are more than an inch thick and big enough to satisfy the appetite of even a three-hundred-pound man like Big Joe Turner. The deep flavor comes from careful tending over the old gas stoves and banks of ovens. The Old South may be a thing of the past, but the charm and tastes from Doe's made me wish that fast food had never intruded into the Delta.

The next day, I drove to Leland to see Son Thomas, who lives on Sinclair Street, across the railroad tracks, down a gravel road, around a corner, and on the right in a three-room, unpainted shotgun house. It was a warm, sunny day, and we moved straight-back wooden chairs out of the front room and onto a small porch. A German shepherd was sleeping under the house, oblivious to the flies and gnats that buzzed around its head. Son played "Catfish Blues" for me, singing unexpurgated lyrics. His voice was light and lyrical. Children wandered up and down the street, stopped for a moment to listen, then walked on, occasionally glancing back as they turned the corner. It seemed no different from the way it must have been fifty years ago when folk-music collectors streamed out of the North to capture the blues on tape for posterity and scholarship. The music hung in the air, its melody curling back on itself like wood smoke from an old stove.

Son Thomas had deep scars on his nose, thin, graying hair, and no front teeth. He was only fifty-eight, but he seemed old enough to remember singing to W. C. Handy about the Southern crossing the Yellow Dog. Between songs, as he tuned his new Martin guitar, he talked about himself and his music.

"I moved here in 1961 from a place called Eden. I used to farm over there, but I couldn't ever make no money farming," Thomas says as he twists the pegs on the neck of his guitar. "I moved here to help my grandfather dig graves. Every time somebody died and they'd be buried around Leland here, he'd get fifteen dollars. But when I first come over, they wasn't dying fast enough and I thought about moving back. My grandaddy only had one arm and he wanted me to stay on. 'Somebody's gonna die,' he said, but I had been here three weeks and ain't nobody died yet."

He plucked each string to see if it was in tune and then continued: "My grandaddy told me I didn't have to worry about eatin' and sleepin' if I'd just stay around and help him dig graves. But I wanted me a drink of whiskey and didn't have no money. And I told him, 'The thing about it is, ain't nobody dying.' Then somebody had a wreck up the road and you could see the ambulance come and then the drivers for the funeral home just going right on out there. And my grandaddy said, 'Whooo, that's liable to be one right there.' I held that job as long as I could. But then they started dying *too* fast and I couldn't hold it no longer. My back started giving me trouble."

Thomas learned to play guitar in his late teens, after listening to his grandfather and uncle. "They played mostly blues," he says, "but my grandfather, he used to play country-and-western music because that's what the white peoples wanted to hear. And I used to listen to the Grand Ole Opry out of Nashville and the radio station out of Cincinnati, Ohio." When he wasn't digging graves, Thomas said, he played in juke joints like the Easy Pay House on Highway 49 between Yazoo City and Eden. That's where he knew legendary bluesmen Elmore James, Arthur "Big Boy" Crudup, and Sonny Boy Williamson. "I used to play Elmore James's guitar some on Saturday night. Elmore, he would take a break and he'd let me play his guitar. And that old harp player with him was Sonny Boy Williamson. And old Sonny Boy would get mad because I was playing Elmore James's guitar. The peoples in there seemed like they enjoyed it, but it would sure make old Sonny Boy mad.

"People playing the blues nowadays are copying behind B. B. King. But not me. He only plays one string. I have all six strings to play. But B.B., he doesn't have to play six. He's got that background that will pick it up. If I'd had somebody to back me up down at the festival yesterday, I wanted to show Albert King he wasn't the onliest somebody that could make runs like that. Some of em, they don't play different tunes like I do. Of course, that's the way it is in country music like the white folks used to play. Today, all these fellas plays all their records to the same tune. But, see, I do a change-up.

"You know, I been to festivals everywhere. Texas, Washington, D. C., Boston, but I ain't never wanted to move out of Mississippi—and I been in lots of places. The only place in the North I seen I thought I could get used to was Washington, D. C. Chicago—I don't want to live there. It's too large a city for me. And I don't like New York. I could never get around there. You really get mixed up in New York City."

As I sat on his porch, listening to him play, Son Thomas conjured up the ghosts of Delta bluesmen like Charley Patton and Robert Johnson, Big Bill Broonzy and Mississippi Fred McDowell. Johnson, of course, is the most famous and—with songs like "Crossroad Blues," "Hellhound on My Trail," and "Me and the Devil Blues"—the most mysterious. He was born in Hazelhurst, Mississippi, which is south of Jackson, on May 8, 1911. At first he was called Robert Dodds. But Charles Dodds, his mother's husband, fled to Memphis to avoid a lynch mob and in his absence, Robert was fathered by Noah Johnson. Robert and his mother, Julia, moved to Memphis a few years later and lived with Charles Dodds and his mistress. That didn't work out. After hanging around Memphis a couple of more years, Robert moved to Robinsonville, Mississippi, to live with his mother and new stepfather. In his teens he got interested in music, moving from the Jew's harp to the harmonica to the guitar. Johnson met and learned the blues from Son House, who had learned from Charley Patton.

Robert Johnson recorded only twenty-seven songs, but his reputation was so great that almost any Delta bluesman who recorded after 1937 listed him as a major influence. And surely phrases from his songs like, "Hello, Satan, I believe it's time to go," "Me and the devil both walkin' side by side," "I can't keep no money, Hellhound on my trail" added a touch of supernatural mystery to his legend, which is the basis for a screenplay, *Love In Vain*, by Alan Greenberg, and a completed movie, *Crossroads*, by John Fusco. Johnson died in 1938 from poisoned whiskey given to him at a houseparty. There were always stories about Johnson selling his soul to the devil at a Delta crossroads to gain his mastery of the blues.

Although Johnson may be the best-known branch in this blues family tree, another man was its trunk, if not its roots. That's Charley Patton, who in 1930 made the first recordings of the Delta blues. In *Blues Who's Who* he is listed as a major influence on the music of Kid Bailey, Dick Bankston, Willie Lee Brown, Honeyboy Edwards, Son House, Howlin' Wolf, Tommy Johnson, Robert Johnson, Floyd Jones, Bertha Lee, Fred McDowell, Johnny Shines, Henry Sims, Roebuck Staples, Eddie Taylor, Muddy Waters, and Bukka White. That's almost as many *begats* as you'll find in the Book of Chronicles in the Old Testament.

Patton, who was born in either 1881, 1885, or 1887, was a scrawny, light-skinned man with wavy hair and Caucasian features. In 1897 his family moved to Dockery Farms, one of the major cotton plantations in the Delta. Patton first learned guitar there. He played with the Chatmon family, who performed mostly dance music for white people. But he also learned from Henry Sloan, a guitarist with a more primitive, gritty sound. It was from that sound that the blues developed. Patton spent a lot of time on Dockery Farms—most of it playing the blues, drinking whiskey, and chasing women. Occasionally, he'd repent and preach a few sermons, but he was always tempted by a guitar and a good time and, in the end, the blues won out. It's hard to trace Robert Johnson—the hellhound on his trail kept him moving—but Patton's roots are easy to find. All you've got to do is follow the Sunflower River to Dockery Farms. When I left Son Thomas I decided to drive over to Dockery, about twenty miles from where the Southern crosses the Yellow Dog, and see what's left from the old days.

Dockery is near Cleveland, about eight miles down Mississippi Route 8, between Highways 61 and 49. Most historians say the Delta blues was born on or near this huge, five-thousand-acre plantation. It's where Patton worked and regularly disappointed his father, a sometimes preacher, by siding with the devil and playing the blues. When Patton lived on Dockery in the 1920s, there were as many as a thousand black people working the cotton fields that curve gently around both banks of the Sunflower River. The plantation was carved out of the canebrake in 1895 by Will Dockery, who became one of the most successful planters in the area. In 1936, Joe Rice Dockery, Will's son, took over. Joe Dockery died in 1983, and his widow, Keith Sommerville Dockery, is in charge now. Mrs. Dockery and I talked in the back room of a defunct gas station with rusted pumps. It serves as the plantation office on the edge of the property. There is a giant sailfish her husband caught mounted on the wall, next to a flag for a New Orleans yacht club. She is an attractive, gracious woman, and she apologizes for her lack of knowledge about the music that originated on her land.

"The first time we started giving much thought to the blues was when some people telephoned Joe and said they understood from reading in the Tulane Library that the blues started here," she says. "Joe said, 'Well, really?' And, I don't know, people just began to call us and this has been going on about twenty years now. It was a revelation even to my husband, Joe, who spent his boyhood here on this plantation. And he used to hunt and fish with these people and they went to school here."

The small, unpainted houses where the workers lived were away from the Dockery home, across the Sunflower River in some cases, and it's easy to see how the Dockerys could be unaware of what was going on in them. "We never had the black people in to play music for us, the way some plantation owners did," Mrs. Dockery says. "We felt that would be, well, sort of demeaning." During the twenties, Dockery Farms had its own railroad—the Pea Vine that Charley Patton sings about—a general store large enough to employ five clerks and sell everything from groceries to coffins; a dock for steamboats; a cotton gin; and two churches.

Most of the "quarters," where Charley Patton grew up and learned to play the blues, have been torn down and plowed under now, and the massive general store is over-grown with kudzu. Mechanized agriculture has reduced the need for field labor. The farm survives, but many of the workers moved north and the old land of cotton re-mains only in the imagination.

"It all just changed gradually," says Mrs. Dockery, "when the mechanical cotton pickers came in and the trac-tors began proliferating. Then the workers became un-happy. They began to realize that the situation wasn't any good for them here. I remember my mother and I used to talk a lot about the black situation and how treacherous we felt it was. We didn't feel it could go on like that and we believed it should not go on. There was an unrest and they began to go north—to Detroit and Toledo and Akron and Chicago—anywhere they could just to get out of Mississippi. That was in the thirties. Joe and I were married in 1938 and I think the place had begun to get smaller then. He farmed it all, although we did have one big general manager and four or five what we called straw bosses. Of course, the term *plantation manager* has a bad connotation because this person was a go-between between the owner and the worker. And this man was here to enforce what he thought was the owner's desires. And with these people, there was not that quality of noblesse oblige. That might not be so good, but maybe some of it's not so bad. The educated people had that and wanted to help the underprivileged and realized the situation. I guess the big exodus was after World War Two.

"But now back to the music. You know, I remember those Saturday nights. They talk so much about Saturday-night brawls and all of that. Now, I remember that. Even as a child. Because my father was a small-town lawyer and he would get these calls in the middle of the night to come and get somebody out of jail and all. He did a lot of charity practice with the blacks. If they got in trouble, he'd go and get 'em out, and chances are he either didn't charge them or charged them very little.

"Now, here on Dockery there were lots of black people. It was a real big community. We would meet people all during Joe's lifetime—people in Memphis or Jackson or New Orleans—and they'd say, 'Oh, I know you, Mr. Dockery, I know you, Mr. Joe. I grew up on Dockery.' And they always said it with kindness and joy. We've always prided ourselves that Joe and his father were kind to everyone and fair. I'm certain that there must have been some plantations where the feeling was not so good. It's just one of those things we don't talk about very much."

Most of the field workers left, but Charley Patton's nephew, Tom Cannon, still lives on the plantation. He's seventy-three, and works as a family retainer. Mrs. Dockery and I drive from the defunct gas station, past the gin and up to her home, a large, rambling bungalow with a swimming pool and tennis courts on the side. Tom Cannon is in the yard, trimming hedges.

"Tom," says Mrs. Dockery, "this is Mr. Merrill from Atlanta, and he wants to talk to you about the blues here on the plantation. Didn't you say you knew Charley Patton?"

"Yessir," Cannon says as he opens and closes the hedge clippers with a nervous rhythm. "Charley Patton, that was my uncle. He went to puttin' out these blues records after he got to be a man and he stayed round here all his days and he was buried down here at Holly Ridge. When he died I was about sixteen years old. He made up his own songs and started off with a guitar and ended up puttin' out records. I never figured he'd be famous until he started puttin' out those records, but he started off as a boy. His daddy moved here from Boulder, Mississippi. Charlie was about ten years old when they moved. My mother was older than he was.

"He was just a blues singer and he'd go 'round and play for these different places. He loved to argue about things. He got cut up over there one time too, for talking to a man's wife. All the ladies loved him. He was light-skinned and he had a real good head of hair, you know, a light-skinned colored man.

"Charley stayed right over north of the place, over

there in a little house with his daddy. He just took up music himself." He pauses, shifts his weight uncomfortably, continues to make the rhythmic noise with the clippers, and finishes his story. "They say everything about him, say the devil taught him to play. He sat down and made his own songs, even made a song about Mister Jeff, the plantation manager. He played lots of music around here, played for different white people. Then some people from over in Robinsonville came to get him and they got him to move over there for about a year, but he wouldn't stay long. Charley and his wife would have rounds, but I don't know if you could call it a fight. I saw him hit her, but she wouldn't hit back. He hit hard. And then she'd leave and he'd go get her or he'd get him another woman. I don't know how many wives he did have. After he got to be a man, he left here and went to Milwaukee and was puttin' out blues records, but he moved back to Holly Ridge. Then he took sick and passed. If ain't nobody messed with his marker, it should be right down there."

"Tom," Mrs. Dockery asks, "how many people do you think lived here when you were a boy?"

"I think there was more than a thousand. I know Mr. Dockery had a hundred cars over on the other side of the river. Back when these Model-T Fords were coming out, I heard Mr. Dockery's daddy bought over a hundred tags for the other side of the river. There were houses all over the place. Yessir, those houses weren't as far apart as from here to that house you see yonder. You see, your house was over on your block of land and you worked thirty acres. I was a little kid, but I remember those boats on the Sunflower River and my dad talkin' about how they brought in so much stuff. My daddy worked in the brick store."

After we finish talking to Tom Cannon, we drive around the plantation in Mrs. Dockery's Mercedes and inspect this year's crop. "You know," she says as we drive across the Sunflower River and back toward the remnants of the once-sprawling quarters, "I had a note from a man who visited us, and he went back to Memphis and he wrote us, 'These little towns, they look so pitiful, don't they?' And I thought to myself, *I drive through these little towns every day and they do look pitiful.* But you get accustomed to it. You know, the afternoon after my husband's death, Tom Cannon's wife came to see me and she said, 'Oh, Mrs. Dockery, I wish you could have been here in the old days, it was so much fun.' "

As I leave Dockery Farms, I remember an old song Charley Patton wrote:

> *They run me from Will Dockery's, took me off my job.*
> *Went out and told Papa Charley*
> *I don't want you hanging 'round my job no more.*
> *Fella, down in the country, it almost make you cry.*
> *Women and children, flaggin' freight trains for rides.*

It was only a short drive from Dockery to Moorehead, the place where the Southern crosses the Yellow Dog. Both Dockery and Moorehead are in Sunflower County. So maybe this really is the Tigris-Euphrates Valley for the blues. Moorehead is a sleepy little town and in midafternoon when I arrived, it was almost deserted. I drove around the square and nobody seemed to be out. But in the center of the square was an abandoned railroad station. I parked there, got out, and walked around. I was about to go ask somebody in one of the stores if they knew where the Southern crossed the Yellow Dog when I saw a historical marker.

In the South, most historical markers commemorate the Civil War. Every battle, march, and retreat are memorialized with one of these plaques. In Selma, Alabama, for example, there are markers all over town certifying that Union or Confederate troops passed this way more than a hundred years before. But there is no mention of the great civil rights march. So I expected this marker to tell me that someone's raiders had marched through when Moorehead was only a canebrake. I was wrong.

WHERE THE SOUTHERN CROSSES THE YELLOW DOG, the lettering said. I looked beyond the marker a few feet and saw, on the ground, a square of railroad track, obscured by weeds. This was it, the earliest known location for the blues. I listened carefully. There was a little rustling of the wind and then, faintly, in the distance, I heard the sounds of Michael Jackson's music from an old radio near the train station. The trains no longer run on the old rusted track that gave the blues a home. And the blues have moved away, too. I got back in the car and drove up Highway 51, past Parchman Farms—the state pen and the subject of a lot of old blues—to Clarksdale.

I checked in at the Holiday Inn.

"How you?" said the desk clerk. "I want you to know that I served the first cup of coffee at the first Holiday Inn in the world when it opened."

"Is that so," I answered, picking up my room key and heading out to the car.

"It sure is. The first one. Just think of that. The first cup of coffee ever served at the first Holiday Inn in America. 'Course I didn't think nothin' of it at the time. It was just another job. But now there's Holiday Inns everywhere. And I served that first cup of coffee."

From the motel, I drove over to the Clarksdale Public Library. Upstairs, there was a blues museum. There were pictures on the wall, taken by an Ole Miss professor of Southern studies named Bill Ferris. Around the room were a lot of books, some old musical instruments, and stacks of records. A decade before, a museum of black history on the Delta probably wouldn't have existed. So even though it was small and reminiscent of an old collection of abandoned stuffed birds, it was a start. I applauded silently and went downstairs to see the librarian.

Willie Lee Brown, Little Willie Foster, Tony Hollins, Earl Hooker, John Lee Hooker, Johnny Moore, Little Junior Parker, Brother John Sellers, and Maxwell Street Jimmy Thomas were all born in Clarksdale. But that's not what makes the town famous in blues history. This is the town where Bessie Smith died, out on Highway 61. The Empress of the Blues was in a review called *Broadway Rastus*, a carnival tent show that had played Memphis the night before. She was to open the next day in Clarksdale. But instead of spending the night in Memphis, she headed south. Just outside of Clarksdale her Packard slammed into a Uneeda biscuit company truck. Her right arm was almost severed, she was bleeding like crazy, and soon after she got to the hospital, the greatest blues singer of all time was pronounced dead.

Bessie's death was as controversial as her life, which was filled with brawls, booze, and lovers both male and female. John Hammond, the Columbia Records producer and sometimes journalist, wrote in *Downbeat* magazine that Bessie Smith had died because she was denied treatment at a white hospital. The 1930s, of course, were the days of institutional racism in the South and the story seemed plausible. Twenty-three years later Edward Albee wrote a play, *The Death of Bessie Smith*, based on Hammond's story. Racism, it seemed, not an automobile accident, caused Bessie's death.

I decided to ask the librarian to help me find the truth. He was a quiet, shy man who looked at me with a hint of suspicion. I introduced myself, explained what I wanted and snapped on my tape recorder. He glanced first at me, than at the recorder.

"Is that a tape recorder?" he asked.

"Sure is," I said.

"Turn it off. Please, turn it off. Just turn it off, if you don't mind." Suddenly he was as pale as Dockery cotton.

Sure, I told him, and switched it off. Then I asked him to tell me the details of Bessie Smith's death. I said that since he was the town librarian and the curator of the Blues Museum, and since Bessie Smith died here, surely he must know the truth.

"I don't care to comment on that," he said. "If you want to know how it happened, I can refer you to a number of books and you can read what various authors have said."

"Look," I said, "I'm not here for scholarship. Surely you can tell me. I mean, was she taken to a white hospital and refused admittance?"

"I'll get the books for you," he said.

As it turned out, Hammond's account was mostly fiction. The doctor who treated Bessie Smith said it was unthinkable, in 1937, that a black woman would be taken to a white hospital. But, he said, the hospitals were only about a half mile apart. So racism didn't kill Bessie, after all.

"Where was that old hospital?" I asked. "And where is the spot on the highway where Bessie Smith was killed?"

He never told me. After a minute or two I left. The fear of past racism and the history it might have made runs deep in Clarksdale. As I left the museum, I picked up a chamber of commerce brochure. Clarksdale, it said, was proud of its blues heritage. In addition to the museum, there was a barbershop in town where an old barber doubled as a blues singer and occasionally served whiskey from his back room, which was a sort of juke joint. I drove by the barber shop but it was closed. I ate a barbecue and drank a beer and went back. Still closed. The next morning, before I left for Helena, Arkansas, I checked again. Closed. The blues in Clarksdale was not open for business.

Charley Patton made his last record in 1934. Seven years later, seventy-five miles away, across the Mississippi River in Helena, Arkansas, a new radio station, KFFA, broadcast the first *King Biscuit Time*—a program that for the next forty years would have almost as much impact on the blues as *The Grand Ole Opry* had on country music.

In the forties, the only way across the river was on a ferry run by Harold Jenkins, country singer Conway Twitty's father. On most days when he piloted the boat from his home in Friar's Point, Mississippi, to Helena, Arkansas, some of his passengers were the musicians who would appear on *King Biscuit Time*, performers like Sonny Boy Williamson and Robert Junior Lockwood. Helena became less remote when a bridge across the river was built in the mid-fifties. Although most of the *King Biscuit Time* performers are dead, Sonny Payne, the staff announcer for the show, is still in Helena, working for KFFA.

Sonny meets me in the radio station on the top floor

of the five-story Helena National Bank building, the tallest in town. Short and stout with dark hair only lightly streaked with gray, he was a big-band bass player with the Charlie Spivak and Ted Weems orchestras, a native of Helena, and the great repository of the lore of *King Biscuit Time*.

"In the thirties, people used to look forward to going down to the train depot to hear the blues," Sonny says. "Back then we had a streamliner—they called it the Doodlebug—that went from here to Memphis. People would gather around the depot to watch the train come in and listen to the blues. The musicians would all be down there or on the seawall, singing and playing. People would gather around to listen and pitch them a sack of marbles, or maybe a sack of Bull Durham tobacco. We had no idea back then what the blues would become—we thought we were the only ones who enjoyed it."

Sonny Boy Williamson usually played in one of a score of nightclubs and restaurants that dotted downtown Helena. When KFFA started, he saw an opportunity. So he and another musician went to see Sam Anderson, who owned the new radio station. Anderson liked the music, but told the two they'd need a sponsor. He sent them to Max Moore, owner of Interstate Grocery. "And Max agreed to sponsor them," Sonny Payne says. "He was the owner of King Biscuit Flour and he had white cornmeal, too. He took a picture of Sonny Boy sitting barefoot on a big tow sack. And they put that picture on the package and it became Sonny Boy Corn Meal."

The show began with Sonny Payne announcing, "Pass the Biscuits! It's *King Biscuit Time*! Light as air! White as snow! That's King Biscuit Flour, the perfect flour for all your baking needs. And remember friends, for the cornbread with the old-fashioned taste appeal, treat your family to Sonny Boy Corn Meal . . . it's white and just right and it's extremely fancy, too!"

King Biscuit Time was on the air Monday through Friday from noon until twelve-thirty. "We had some of the highest-class people in society in Phillips County listening to *King Biscuit Time*," Sonny Payne says. "I'm talking about bankers and bigwigs like that. They loved the blues, just loved it. And if we didn't go on the air right on time, they called and wanted to know what's going on. Some of your ladies in the beauty shop, they'd call and say, 'Hey, get Sonny Boy to play so-and-so.'

"I'd say twice a month we had to get Sonny Boy out of the clink. It was usually for drinking or fighting—he never stabbed anybody that I know of. Now, Sonny Boy had a heart of gold, but at the same time he was meaner than hell to his own people. There was no such thing as performing without a snootful, and every day he would have a little taste before he came up to play. But he wasn't drunk or irrational. He was a temperamental blues musician. He never wrote down a song in his life. He made it up as he went along. Sometimes I'd ask him, 'What are you gonna sing?' And he'd say, 'I dunno.' And I'd say, 'What do you mean you don't know? I've got to have something to tell these people.' Then he'd say, 'Oh, I know one I went over in my head last night.' And that's what he'd sing. Sonny Boy made fifteen dollars a week, which was pretty good money back then. All in all, he sold enough flour and meal to make him a rich man, and he died broke. He was by far a cut above all the others. He was the best phraser in the business, the best musician.

"Now let me put it this way. Sonny Boy was the type of person that if he loaned you a dollar or whatever—for the most part, we were always loaning Sonny Boy a dollar—but if he loaned you some money and you told him you were gonna pay it back tomorrow, he expected the dollar back the next day. . . . He'd sing, 'I had a friend of mine ask me for four hundred dollars and I didn't have but three hundred ninety-nine.' I said, 'What'd you tell him that for?' He said, 'That way, I didn't have to loan him any money.' That's the way he was. He was a real rascal. One time he got in trouble with a fella who had played with him," Sonny Payne says. "Sonny Boy owed the man some money and when he paid off, the man said he would buy Sonny Boy a drink. Then the fella changed his mind and wouldn't. So Sonny Boy just picked up a beer bottle and cold-cocked him, just because the man wouldn't buy him a drink.

"We used to go down to Wahbash and Elaine [Arkansas] to promote the flour and the meal. He was straight when he went out on the promotional tours. Mr. Moore and Sam insisted on that. We used to play at the Plaza Theater, promoting grocery stores. It was an all-black theater. We'd tell him, 'Stay straight while you're up. When you're through playing, I don't care if you drink the town dry.' And he was pretty straight for the most part. Now, as far as being in the studio up here, he'd quaff a few and that was it. He'd play his thing, get his rocks off, and then he was gone again."

We left the radio station and drove around Helena for a while, mostly in the black section. "There were at least eight restaurants in this section of town which I'll show you," Sonny Payne said. "They're not all here now. Most of 'em closed or burnt down. And these places would have a night club, so to speak, and Sonny Boy played in and around these places all the time. Then, on the weekends, you had your country blues singers. The black people who worked in the country came by horse and buggy and they came by Model A, and they would gather down here and set up on the corner and they would sing and play. They'd say, 'Anything y'all want to drop in, we'd appreciate.' It was their way of making extra money. But Sonny Boy, music was all he did. He'd play the nightclubs and he made enough to keep him going. He'd stay in this rooming house over here across the street for about two dollars a week.

He was the best musician in the business and he couldn't even read a note. He didn't even understand what a note meant. He didn't know what improvisation meant. He didn't understand anything about that. Sonny Boy was a creator. He was the creator of music and blues. He was a cut above the people who came from the farms, but these people were top-dog, too. These people were no slouches.

"Speaking of these people who came to town on weekends, they were the type who would make their songs up and they would sing about their ancestors and about work on the farm. They would sing about the wagons they drove all day or a team of mules. This is what we call typical Southern blues. These people were just amusing themselves and letting it all hang out.

"Lightnin' Hopkins came up here one time. He's dead now, bless his heart. He could scarcely see anymore that last time I saw him. He had cataracts all over him, on his eyes. This was ten, twelve, maybe fourteen years ago. My secretary came in and said, 'There's a Mister Albert Hopkins to see you.' And I said, 'Who? I don't know any Albert Hopkins. Who is he?' And she said, 'Well, he's real old, some black man.' And I said, 'That must be Lightnin'.' And he came in and we talked about the time he played down at the Plaza Theater with Sonny Boy. He made one last appearance with the gang before they all kicked off.

"There was only one type of Southern blues, and that's the type we created in the Delta. You know, I was a musician, and I went off for a while and came home in fifty-three. You know, I had no idea there'd ever be this interest in the blues, no idea at all. Nobody else did either. I mean, even when Sonny Boy went off to tour Europe, we didn't have any earthly idea about it. We thought we're the only ones in the world who enjoy it. Surely nobody else would like this junk. Well, it really wasn't junk. But we took everything for granted."

Sonny Boy became known as the best blues harmonica player in the country. Eventually he moved to Detroit, made scores of records, and toured Europe.

"His attitude changed once he got to be famous," Sonny Payne said. "He was still on the booze and I never knew him to be on drugs. But he was a very heartbroken man." Then, unexpectedly, he returned to Helena in the fall of 1964.

"Sonny Boy was a very broken man when he came home," Sonny Payne says. "He looked like a boxer who had been through a meat grinder. You take a man—he may have been a mean son of a bitch, but at the same time he was one hell of a man—and he knows what it's like on top and now he's on the bottom. It just breaks his spirit. He came up to the station and he stood and looked me in the eye and I knew he was a dead man. I asked him what he was doing home, and he said, 'Ahhh, Mister Sonny, I'm tired. I got everybody paid off. I owe Mister

Sam five dollars and I'm gonna pay him right now. But I really came home to die and I'm gonna be buried at home.' And I said, 'Only God knows when you're gonna die.' And he looked at me with those big eyes and he said, 'I know, too.' That was so weird. He lived eight months more, maybe nine. I keep remembering those big eyes. He was just beat up and tired. People took advantage of him, particularly the agents, the people who booked him. I know one who just ripped him off all to pieces. He went to live upstairs over the Dreamland Café. And then he was dead."

King Biscuit Time went off the air in 1982, when Interstate Grocery closed. For the last few years, the show limped along. "The musicians started drifting away and the nightclubs started closing," Sonny Payne says. "A lot of them were frustrated because they couldn't make a living. So they drifted off to Memphis and up north. Robert Junior [Lockwood] has been gone fifteen years. Francis Clay, he went off to Chicago about ten or twelve years ago, but he came back and he's working for some farmer in Elaine. Houston Stackhouse died, and his son works out here at the Country Club. About eighty percent of the musicians were dying off and the young people didn't want to play the blues, didn't want to capitalize on it. At the end, we were just playing records. There weren't any people to play. There was nothing left to make it interesting anymore."

I leave Helena, listening to KFFA. It's a country station now. As I drive down Cherry Street, I wonder about a theory I heard that claims everything ever played on the air can someday be captured again. If that's true, the voice of Sonny Boy Williamson is still somewhere in the ether singing:

Good evenin' everybody,
tell me how do you do?
We're the King Biscuit Boys
and we've come out to play for you.
We're sellin' King Biscuit Flour,
money-back guarantee.
And if you find you don't like it,
send it on back to me.

2

WHEN THE BLUES FIRST left home and moved from the Delta into the consciousness of America, it went to Memphis. Any road map will tell you Memphis is in Tennessee. Geographically, I suppose, that's correct. But a cultural map would show Memphis as the largest city in Mississippi, the capital of the Delta. Cotton was the backbone of the economy there as well, but in Memphis it was the commerce of cotton, not the growing of it. If Memphis represented the society that grew up along the fertile banks of the Mississippi, it was more sophisticated than in the Mississippi small towns. For whites, there was no surer way to meet old friends than to sit in the lobby of the Peabody Hotel. That was the cultural center of planter society, a place where, it's been said, if you wait long enough you'll see everyone from the Delta. I had reservations for a night there. I crossed the bridge at Helena, drove back into Mississippi and then straight up Highway 61.

Memphis is the home of W. C. Handy, whom it heralds as The Father of the Blues. It was also the home of the jug band. Blues was part of the jug-band repertoire, along with popular songs and old country ditties. In the mid-1920s Memphis was a center of vaudeville, and the related medicine shows which featured groups like the Memphis

Jug Band and Cannon's Jug Stompers. The Memphis Jug Band was started by a street singer named Will Shade, who played up and down Beale Street and then graduated to medicine shows. Shade was a solo act until the night he met a man named "Roundhouse" Beale. "Roundhouse" asked if he could play with Shade and he picked up a bottle and started blowing on it. People at the bars started shouting, "Jug Band, Jug Band." There had been jug bands before, of course, the most notable being the Clifford Hayes Dixie Jug Blowers from Louisville. "Roundhouse" vanished after that first innovative night, but Shade got another jug blower and a kazoo player the next day and the band was formed.

A year later, in 1928, after the jug band had become popular enough to spawn such imitators as the Beale Street Jug Band and the South Memphis Jug Band, a medicine-show veteran named Gus Cannon, who played a banjo made from his mother's biscuit pan covered with a raccoon skin, formed his Jug Stompers. The guitarist with the Jug Stompers was Furry Lewis. Furry was an old hand at medicine shows. He's played with "doctors" like Dr. C. E. Hangerson and Dr. W. B. Milton throughout the South, pushing tonics and remedies to the gullible. Eventually, as a solo recording artist, Furry Lewis became as well known as the jug bands and his country blues became indigenous to Memphis. Furry Lewis, Gus Cannon, and Will Shade are all dead now and few celebrate their music. When Memphis talks about the blues, they talk about W. C. Handy or the early days of Sun Records.

Before I left for Memphis I arranged to meet Joe Savarin, the executive director of the Blues Institute—an organization that sounded scholarly and substantial. Every time I called him, I had to deal with what sounded like a huge switchboard. Memphis, it seems, takes the blues seriously. Just across the Mississippi line there are roadside signs for Beale Street, made famous in the early blues years by W. C. Handy. Memphis advertises itself as the home of the blues, and as I drove into town, I was looking forward to hearing good music and talking late into a smoky night with, if not The Father of the Blues, at least its great-uncle.

There may be government-sponsored roadside signs for Beale Street, but in truth, the blues is not what Memphis means anymore. Memphis means Elvis. Nothing there can compare to his shrine—Graceland, Presley's plantation of bad taste. But it is more than a shrine, it's an industry. There is a full shopping center across the street from the antebellum-style mansion filled with Elvis souvenirs. And they're cheap only by appearances. A cookie jar in the shape of a pink Cadillac, for example, sells for forty dollars. When I stopped at the shopping center, there was a display of paintings of Presley done by his fans. To many of the artists, he has become Oriental and inscrutable. His eyes are narrowed to slits and there is the heavy weight of excess flesh on his cheeks. He looks like a sideburned Buddha. But maybe that's just the inevitable effect of using black velvet rather than canvas.

There are a number of Elvis impersonators waiting in line to tour Graceland, and I wondered if there would be B. B. King and Howlin' Wolf look-alikes downtown. I wondered if perhaps Memphis was a swirl of has-beens and would-bes all dressed like fallen idols, waiting for the spirit to enter and make them the King for a Day. But downtown, as I checked in, people seemed normal enough. The costumes were confined to the faithful at Graceland.

Joe Savarin called me at the Peabody. "I'll meet you on a bench in Handy park in thirty minutes," he said. "I'll be the one in Bermuda shorts with a gray beard." Somehow, I expected the executive director of the Blues Institute to wear a three-piece suit. A half hour later, I was at Handy Square, a park on Beale Street built around a statue of W. C. Handy. A small crowd waited silently for a bus, but none of them wore shorts or had a gray beard. I walked around. Beale Street was in the midst of restoration. Developers decided to regenerate it as a Bourbon Street North and there were a few clubs here and there, plus a sort of fast-food barroom with piña coladas and Hurricanes on tap. The street was empty and quiet. If Beale Street could talk, it wouldn't have much to say.

Still no man in shorts showed up. I glanced at my watch. He was fifteen minutes late. The park was empty. I walked across the street and talked to a man in a makeshift shoeshine parlor.

"Where's the Blues Institute?"

"Say what?"

"The Blues Institute, I'm supposed to meet someone from there."

"Hmmm. I don't know anything about a Blues Institute . . . wait a minute. I think that's it over there." He pointed to a blue plywood box. "That's the only thing I can figure it might be. Shine, Mister?"

I walked away. *What a fool*, I think. Trying to say a cheap plywood box no bigger than a couple of refrigerator crates could be the prestigious Blues Institute of Memphis. A loudspeaker somewhere played Dave Brubeck, great jazz but a poor imitation of the blues. The notes bounced off the empty street.

In the distance, I saw a man walking toward the park. He was wearing Bermuda shorts, a yellow T-shirt that read, I (heart) THE BLUES—and jogging shoes. He had a white beard. It was Joe Savarin. "Sorry I'm late," he said breathlessly, and immediately began what sounded like a prepared speech on the history of the blues. The blues didn't start in Mississippi, *nosiree*. It was right here in Memphis on Beale Street, a fine street with some of the best homes and churches, the finest theaters, and best restaurants. Yessir, right here on Beale Street is where—let's walk this way—follow me please—where a great American art form was born.

He sounded like a carnival barker, and he is wrong about Beale. W. C. Handy wrote about a good-time street with women of easy virtue, plenty of whiskey, and a hint of violence. The street described by the director of the Blues Institute was as safe, clean, and middle-class as Disneyland.

When Savarin finished his spiel, standing beneath a statue of Elvis Presley, he told me a little about himself. He was a promoter in Biloxi and Gulf Port, hawking strippers and musicians and planning outrageous publicity schemes for failing movie stars. Then he came to Memphis, founded the Blues Institute and started the annual Blues Awards show where the W. C. Handy Awards are given out for the year's best performances. Other than Miss Nude America, it's probably the only awards show in the country without a national television contract. He is also raising money to buy a defunct theater and make it a permanent tourist attraction like the Country Music Hall of Fame in Nashville. If I'll follow him, he said, we'll drop by his office and he'll give me some literature. We walked down Beale and he began rustling the keys in his pocket as we approached the blue plywood box. He opened the door, edged around the counter where he sells Cokes to tourists, and gathered up some programs and posters. I bought the posters, we shook hands and promised to keep in touch.

Back at the Peabody, I sat back and thought about Memphis and the blues. In the early twentieth century, Memphis prided itself on being more cosmopolitan than any other city in the South. There was an opera house at the corner of Main and Beale, there were the "good-time houses on front street" Tennessee Williams wrote about, and on Beale itself, there was the Palace Theater. The Palace was the town's black showplace, and any musician who worked there knew how to read music, how to play show tunes, and uptown dance melodies. The Palace was the local home of acts provided by the Theater Owner's Booking Association, the major black vaudeville talent provider. It was called the TOBA, which performers said meant "tough on black asses." Included with comic acts like Butterbeans and Susie were the classic blues singers —Ma Rainey, Ida Cox, Clara Smith, Sippie Wallace, Victoria Spivey, Ethel Waters, Mamie Smith, Alberta Hunter, and of course, the Empress of the Blues, Bessie Smith herself.

The classic blues had little to do with the sounds of the Delta. Instead of guitars, the singers were backed with jazz bands, a sort of Dixieland ensemble, or, when they played New York, a more sophisticated group like the Fletcher Henderson orchestra. The raw, folk-sound of the blues was gone and in its place was an uptown show business that W. C. Handy understood. Memphis offered urban charm, not an extension of home. And its music, although it may have originated in a tenant-farmer's shack not a hundred miles away, reflected New York more than Dockery Farms. I knocked back my drink and went out into the night, looking for what now passes for the Memphis blues.

I ended up at Blues Alley to see Little Laura Dukes. Her father was a drummer with W. C. Handy's band and in 1913 she was a dancer on Beale Street before it became sanitized. By the 1930s, she was touring with Robert Nighthawk, the legendary blues guitarist. Little Laura was singing when I walked in. Her voice was still strong, and as she sang she offered bumps and grinds like a diminutive Gypsy Rose Lee. In the midst of her gyrations, she glances at her watch, signals the band this is the last chorus, finishes the song, and walks off. There is something cynical about her performance. It is as if she were the last surviving minstrel star, still rolling her eyes and smacking her lips for the white folks who come downtown to see the darkies and their natural rhythm. I finished my drink and left. As I passed the bar, I heard someone say, "That old nigger woman sure can sing." No wonder Little Laura has the blues.

As I walked back to my hotel, I realized Memphis never was the home of the blues, no matter what the chamber of commerce says. It's the city where the blues was transformed and made palatable to a white audience. W. C. Handy heard the blues in Mississippi, came back to Memphis, and rewrote the music in a white style that made it popular. Handy's blues was a variant of Dixieland and ragtime, and much of what was called blues in the early part of the century was really Tin Pan Alley tunes, black music made white and performed on Broadway in shows

like the *Club Harlem Review, Change Your Luck, Creole Follies,*
and *Darktown Scandals.*

I thought about an interview in *Hear Me Talkin' to Ya*
by Nat Shapiro and Nat Hentoff with Buster Bailey, a
Memphis clarinet player:

> We were playing in Memphis at the same time
> they were playing in Storyville in New Orleans.
> The difference was that the New Orleans bands
> did more improvising. Ours was more the note
> variety. We played from the sheets. Ours were
> just dance bands. Fellows that played the circus
> were the top musicians of the day and, during the
> off season, a lot of them would play in the local
> bands like those led by Handy.

On the popular *Believe It or Not* radio program, the
host, Robert Ripley, said Handy originated jazz music.
That claim was disputed by Jelly Roll Morton who said that
Handy not only didn't invent jazz or blues, but copied
"Memphis Blues" from a song written by a New Orleans
pianist named Black Butts. "Butts was strictly a blues player
with no knowledge of music," Morton said, telling an in-
terviewer:

> "Please do not misunderstand me," Morton was
> quoted as saying in "Jazz Masters of New Orleans"
> by Martin Williams, "I do not claim any of the
> creation of the blues, although I have written
> many of them even before Mr. Handy had any
> blues published. I heard them when I was knee-
> high to a duck. Of course, Handy played mostly
> violin when I first arrived in Memphis. Violinists

weren't known to play anything illegitimate even in New Orleans."

And T-Bone Walker, the great Texas bluesman, doubted Handy created the form. "Now you take a piece like 'St. Louis Blues,'" he said in *Hear Me Talkin' to Ya*. "That's a pretty tune and it has a kind of bluesy tone, but that's not the blues. You can't dress up the blues."

In his autobiography Handy said:

The blues is a thing deeper than what you'd call a mood today. Like the spirituals, it began with the Negro, it involves our history, where we came from and what we experienced. In the First World War, all Americans got a taste of what we had had for years—people being torn from their families and sent to faraway places, sometimes against their wishes. And blues and jazz began to have more meaning for more people. Then the depression was a new experience for many. But we had been hungry for years and we had known hunger and hurt.

I decided to walk back toward Beale Street to see if it was any more lively at night. And as I walked, I thought about latter-day blues in Memphis.

In the fifties, the blues came to Memphis when performers like Howlin' Wolf and Ike Turner recorded for Sam Phillips's Sun Records. Phillips had the first recording studio in town and, in addition to recording speeches and novelty items, searched out the black music he'd learned to love in his hometown, Florence Alabama. The recordings he made of Ike Turner, B. B. King, Howlin' Wolf, and others were sold to small labels in Los Angeles and Chicago.

Although he liked the blues, Phillips was looking for a white boy who could combine the sounds of rhythm and blues with country music. It was the era when white parents were still reluctant to let their children listen to "race" music. There were plenty of blues singers in Memphis, particularly in the black suburb of West Memphis, Arkansas. The music's popularity grew because of programming on the all-black WDIA, a radio station where B. B. King was a disc jockey. And yet none of the bluesmen coming through Memphis in the 1950s stayed around long. The record companies they recorded for were in Chicago, and that's where they headed.

Ultimately, Phillips discovered Elvis Presley and then Jerry Lee Lewis, Carl Perkins, and Johnny Cash. He transformed the blues into rock and roll for white teenagers in the same way W. C. Handy changed it from a raw folk sound to music for white dance bands. It was Elvis who symbolized Memphis now, not B. B. King or Howlin' Wolf. The blues had left town years before and now, with smoke and mirrors, the city fathers were trying to recreate an era in a way it never was.

I stopped in for another bourbon at one of the clubs. I was the only customer. No music was playing. I decided to give Rufus Thomas a call. Thomas, who is in his seventies, has been in Memphis almost all his life. He played the old *Rabbit Foot Minstrels*, worked as a blues deejay, made a couple of bluesy records like "The Funky Chicken," and had seen the music go from Sun records to the soul sounds of Stax. The promotional veneer on Beale was too thick. Maybe Rufus Thomas could set me straight.

Rufus Thomas has white hair now and there are wrinkles on his face, but he still qualifies for the title he gives himself, "The World's Oldest Teenager." He was excited over talking about Memphis and the blues, and in a long conversation that lasted late into the night his enthusiasm never flagged.

"When I was eighteen years old I was a tap dancer with the *Rabbit Foot Minstrels*," Thomas remembered. "They were musicals. Chorus girls, comics, that sort of thing. It was a musical review. You had an opening with the chorus girls and all, and right behind that came either the comic or a singer or a dancer. There is a difference today. There is no variety. None. Everybody sings. With the *Rabbit Foot* show, our winter quarters were in Port Gibson, which is way down there in Mississippi. Then we played parts of Arkansas and Mississippi but very little of Tennessee. We played Hernando, Mississippi, which is close to Memphis, but we never played Memphis itself . . . Later on, I was with the *Royal American Shows*, which was a tent-show carnival, and it played Memphis every year during the month of May.

"Of course it was strange at that time. We had black entertainers and all, but it was a segregated show with *Royal American*. And black people didn't come. It was black people performing for white people, but the black patronage was not welcome.

"With *Rabbit Foot*, it was a segregated show, but it was different. On one side was white, on the other side was black, and they had an aisle right down the middle that separated the audience. But there was never a problem.

All of those small towns we played had a square up in the middle of the town. And, up around noon, we would parade around the square. You know, to show some of the stuff we had so the people would come out. It was a sort of a visual advertising. And you'd see a few people on the square, not many. Then you'd wonder where in the world those people came from that night. Man, they all came out of the cotton patches. All out from the thickets and the woods. And they would pack that old tent—a big old tent like a circus tent; and sometimes they'd be so full they had to let up the sides of the tent. But we had great shows and great audiences.

"You had one blues singer in the show. I can't remember her name right now. But I can remember this: There was a real pretty girl sittin' right down front one night—I don't know what town we were in. The chorus girls came out and did all them high kicks and all that. And when they finished, this pretty girl in the audience did just a little applause. Then came a singer. A pretty singer. Man, it was the whole nine yards. Well, the singer came out and sang. When she finished, just a little applause. Then the dancer came out. Still not much. But there was a blues singer on that show and the minute that blues singer started singing them blues, that chick jumped up out of her seat, started to poppin' her fingers, had her dress above her knees. Boy, and she went. She turned herself aloose. And that was in 1937.

"Now they've gone and fixed up Beale Street," Thomas said. "Well, we didn't expect for Beale Street to be like it used to be anyway. Everybody goes to Beale Street now. But during the old days, the clientele on Beale Street was black. Whites went down only on special occasions like the *Midnight Rambles*. When a road show would come to the Palace Theater, which was the show-place of the South, they would have matinees and two night shows. But on Thursday they'd have a third show at midnight that was for whites. They add a little spice to it. Have the girls to strip and when they get right to the point, the lights would go out. You never saw anything. They'd tell spicy jokes and that sort of thing. That's what made it the *Midnight Rambles*. That was the only night the whites came. Now, there was white-owned businesses on Beale but a black clientele. This show was very little different from the *Rabbit Foot Minstrels*. They just called the *Rabbit Foot* show minstrels. It was really vaudeville. Now the old minstrel: I did that in high school at Booker Washington. You know, everybody sitting down and Mister Bones says, 'Who was that lady I saw you with last night?' . . . you know, that sort of thing.

"W. C. Handy had gone to New York by that time. But he used to come back to Memphis every year. In prep football, the winner of the Memphis championship would play a team from another area like Chattanooga or Nashville. And that was called the Blues Bowl. W. C. Handy would come down every year for the game and play that golden trumpet. That's how I happened to meet him. And he was some kind of a man. He was a personality that you would not believe. Mild manners. Didn't seem to get excited about anything, but very warm.

"But, talking about Beale Street—every neighborhood had its roughness, and Beale Street was no worse than any other. You didn't have to go to Beale Street to die from a killing. But the collection of people that went to Beale Street was different. Beale was not a rich-man's neighborhood. Nobody on Beale, the clientele, were rich. Now, they wore good clothes. They wore the best clothes that money could buy. Shoes shined to the bone—and whatever dress was fashionable at that time. Both men and women dressed up. The clothes I remember, they called 'em drapes. They had all those pleats in the front and the pants legs were small at the bottom. They had big hats and they wore a long watch chain and they used to stand on the corner and twirl that chain. It was the zoot suit, the drape, we called it. I went on the radio, WDIA in the 1950s, and Beale Street was still flourishing. Then it started falling apart. They put boards up to the store fronts and it seems like overnight it just went. It was no more.

"Talking about blues singers, now," Thomas said, "Bessie Smith and all of 'em was when I was a kid. There were three, maybe four, that came to Memphis when I was a kid. Let me see here: There was Bessie Smith, there was Mamie Smith, then there was another one called Ida Cox. Now, she was *my* blues singer, I liked her better than I did the rest of them. Bessie got the name, but to me, Ida Cox was the best. Then came one called Memphis Minnie and then came Ma Rainey, then another woman who called herself Ma Rainey number two. Now those were the women blues singers, and there hadn't been anybody who could top those type people except one who I would rate now as a mammoth blues singer—and that's Koko Taylor. She's from Memphis, you know. Strong, big voice. But you don't find as many women nowadays who's singing the blues.

"Now in West Memphis, across the bridge, you're talking the blues language. Howlin' Wolf was on the radio over there. Howlin' Wolf had a fifteen-minute show on KWAM radio. Ain't nothing in West Memphis now. Eighth Street used to be the place in West Memphis. The Little Brown Jug—I used to go over there, boy. It was a joint. They did a lot of gamblin' and stuff over there. But it was the place. It was wide open. I used to work over there in a club with my little band called the Bearcats. Then this sheriff came along and broke that shit up. Broke it up, man. A sheriff named Culp. He was awful. But he didn't pick 'em. If you were white and screwed up, he kicked your butt. If you were black and screwed up he would kick your butt. Didn't make no difference to Culp. He'd just whip on you if you screwed up. He cleaned it up and it wasn't no more fun, man.

"There was some of that stuff on Beale Street of course, years ago, but not like it was in West Memphis. That was back when you had Pee Wee's and the Monarch and two other little joints down on Beale. It wasn't a nightclub, just little gambling joints where people go in and drink. Bar-type situation, smoky, that sort of thing. There's not a lot of blues being played on Beale today. Actually, you can hear more outside the clubs than inside. There's Rum Boogie, they play the blues. And then there's a club with a big old neon sign that says BLUES. That's Club Handy. On Tuesday night they have disco. Not blues.

"I started with Sun Records, maybe about 1951. We were around Sun for a while, and all of the people there were black. The first hit record that came out of Sun Records, I did it. 'Bearcat.' They had a couple of others they leased to Chess Records out of Chicago—records by Howlin' Wolf and Ike Turner. Ike Turner did "Rocket 88." He's from Clarksdale, Mississippi, and he was playing piano at the time. That 'Rocket 88' was a big record for

Sun. But that came after 'Bearcat.' 'Bearcat' was an answer to Big Mama Thornton's 'Hound Dog.' And Sam Phillips tried to get away with not paying for it, because Duke Peacock owned the song with Mama Thornton. So Sam had to pay some royalties for the song. Because it's just like 'Hound Dog'—the same thing. Lot of people thought it was me getting sued but it was Sam.

"Now at that time," Thomas said, "the Wolf was more West Memphis. Of course, Wolf did play Memphis. Howlin' Wolf drew more people in a club than anybody that's ever been in town. There was a club there called the Paradise, and they'd have a thousand, maybe two thousand people. But Howlin' Wolf had 'em hanging off the rafters. He had maybe five thousand people in a two-thousand-seat house. Everywhere you could see was people. And we had another big old club that, like the Paradise, was formerly a skating rink. The Paradise wasn't on Beale, but this other club was, and at this second club—I can't remember the name of it—Howlin' Wolf drew more people than Ray Charles.

"At Sun Records, during that time, the stable was all black. I guess I got treated pretty well. I got some money. But for a black person, when Sam Phillips hired Elvis and those people, it was all over. First Elvis, who could sing black, and then came along Jerry Lee Lewis and Carl Perkins and Johnny Cash. He dropped everybody black like they were a hot potato. And we were developing a Memphis blues sound. They say that once he got white people, it was the beginning of rock and roll. But we were already doing it. It was already there. Joe Turner had rock and roll long before these white people came. Chuck Berry—Little Richard—a direct copy of Little Richard was Jerry

Lee Lewis. Listen to the piano that Jerry Lee Lewis plays —then listen to the piano that Little Richard played back in the 1950s. Identical. Jerry Lee is a copy. So was Elvis in the beginning. So were all of them.

"Whites take it, they take it from somebody black. You find in the fifties the white boy who used to fall to his knees and lay all back and play his horn. Bill Haley. There was already a black man doing that. We been doing that all the time. I saw this black fellow come out of the Hyde Park Theater in Memphis. It was on Chelsea in North Memphis. He walked down the street a half block playing and came back and had people following him like the piper and he walked right back in the theater, the band was still playing, and he picked up the beat and went right on. He used to have lights on his horn and everything. But no recognition. There just was no room out there for recognition at that time. But as soon as the white boys started doing it, the same thing, nothing but direct copy, it became a hit. This fellow who wears the white buck shoes, Pat Boone—all of his songs that made hits for him were cover songs from blacks. And they weren't as good. Hell, no, they weren't near as good.

"And that, I guess, leads up to Stax Records. And that was a whole 'nother ball game. I made the first record for Stax, too. My daughter, Carla, and I with 'Cause I Love You,' had the first hit record for Stax. Now, people called it soul music but it had the blues flavor. Otis Redding. He had the blues flavor. But it wasn't strictly blues. See, they consider the blues to be twelve bars. Or eight bars. Or sometimes fourteen bars, according to who's playing it. I mean they just stretch it out there. But the soul came from voices like Otis. 'Course there was a church feeling to it.

Gospel music is the foundation of it all. I don't mean this current contemporary stuff. I don't mean that at all. I like to hear the true gospel that our people sang years ago in slavery. Spirituals. The good stuff. The blues runs parallel with that.

"When an individual felt deprived of something, he would say, 'Oh, Lord!' And then that fellow down the street who wasn't spiritual would sing the blues. 'Oh, my baby. Somebody help me find my girl!' Same thing. Different words. Now you see what I'm saying. It just follows a pattern there. You got gospel, you got blues, and you got soul. You got a combination of things.

"But the blues never left home. Blues will always be at home. Now, the other stuff left home. Jazz and all of that. Even the gospel left home. But not the blues. Now with Stax, you didn't have what you'd call a strong blues singer on there. I think I was the closest. Then, later on, came Albert King and then Johnny Taylor, who used to be with the Soul Stirrers. When Sam Cook passed, Johnny took his place. And you can still hear the Soul Stirrers in his voice.

"You know, there aren't very many white people who can sing the blues. Janis Joplin could. White people can play the blues but not sing it. Some of these white boys do turn you off when they start to sing. But, Lord, they can play. Like Anson Funderburgh. The boy is notorious. Awesome on a guitar. But Sam Myers is doing the singing. And Sam Myers is black.

"Memphis today—there's not a real whole lot going on. You get special events like Memphis in May and the Beale Street Festival. But unless something like that is going on, there's not a whole lot happening. After they pumped that money into Beale Street, they brought a fellow out of Nashville who used to be in Memphis. Paid all that money and he's gone back to Nashville. That was Chips Moman. And you know, when he came there, his first project was a record with Roy Orbison, Jerry Lee, Carl Perkins, and Johnny Cash. Which to me was just shit for Memphis music," Thomas said. "Not taking anything away from those people because they're country and they're good at their craft. Carl Perkins is closer to blues than any of them. Chips Moman did nothing for Memphis music. Memphis is always coming up with shit like that. They just do it wrong. I don't have no idea why they can't see farther than the end of their nose. The powers that be is who I'm talking about.

"But I'm still with WDIA. Every Saturday morning from six until ten playing the blues. We were doing so good from that slot that we eventually played blues all day on Saturday. Memphis is blues and gospel. I have no idea why you can't hear more blues on the radio. The blues is here to stay. They can't give me a reason why they won't program it. It's bullshit if you say it won't sell. But you wouldn't have blues if all you wanted was a young black audience. Because the young blacks are not playing blues. They're playing this rap stuff or the Michael Jackson or the Prince. The young black has gone away from his roots. Simply gone away.

"Back in the days of rhythm and blues, that's when we appreciated our roots. But now some black people are saying we don't want anything to remind us of yesterday, or the history of earlier times. Hell, that's what keeps you going, in my book—knowing that you don't want to go back to those times again. So you keep working so you won't. There should be something always there to remind you of the reason to go on. Something like the blues."

I left Thomas and headed back to the hotel. I stopped for a few minutes at the railroad terminal and watched people board the midnight train to Chicago. That's where the blues went after the great Memphis assimilation.

3

I DRIVE NORTH FROM Memphis on Highway 51, through Tennessee and Kentucky. It looks like an agricultural no-man's-land—a scrub-crop buffer between the Delta and the Midwest's fabled bread basket. After I cross the Ohio River into Illinois on the rickety old bridge at Cairo, the wheat fields I see are as flat and endless as a golden ocean. A few blacks who migrated north stopped in Cairo, but most kept going until they reached Chicago's South Side. That's why there's no Bloomington Blues, no Kankakee Stomp, no Rantoul Breakdown. Back in Jackson, Stewart Madison compared blues with bluegrass, and, in some ways he's right. Both are played by poor people, both are Southern, and both are outside the mainstream of popular music. But there's a difference. Bluegrass is nostalgic, optimistic, and white. The blues is rough, often threatening, and black. "Bluegrass gave television the *Beverly Hillbillies*," someone once told me, "but can you imagine instead, a bunch of black Mississippi sharecroppers who struck oil and came west just a pickin' and a scowlin'?"

Blues musicians weren't the only blacks who left Mississippi, stopped for a cup of coffee in Memphis, and then headed north. After World War I, a steady stream of people left the plantations for more lucrative industrial jobs. *The Chicago Defender*, for years the most influential black newspaper in the country, ran front-page stories about the need for workers in the Windy City. MORE POSITIONS OPEN THAN MEN FOR THEM, one headline read. The paper contrasted high wages and freedom in Chicago against lynchings, segregation, and indentured servitude in the South. Nobody said the streets near Lake Michigan were paved with gold, but to a lot of Mississippians laboring under the burden of a sharecropper's debt or fifty-cents-a-day wages, it must have seemed that way. By 1930, there were more Mississippi natives living in Chicago than in any other non-Mississippi town.

As the musicians moved north, they transformed the gritty, acoustical country blues into the sharp, electrical urban music heard in South Side clubs like The Casbah, Kitty's Corner, and Theresa's. In the 1960s Chicago blues became the musical roots for the English rock bands playing in this country. Middle-aged blues musicians like Howlin' Wolf and Muddy Waters, almost unknown outside the ghettos, became overnight sensations among white teenagers because they were opening acts for The Rolling Stones and The Beatles. Today, Howlin' Wolf, Little Walter, Muddy Waters, and Jimmy Reed, bastions of the first generation of musicians who moved north from Mississippi, are dead. Willie Dixon, the most prolific blues songwriter in the 1940s and 1950s, has moved to California. Koko Taylor, Magic Slim, and Son Seals, all transplanted Southerners, are now the old-timers who dominate the blues in Chicago. But in most of the city's more than thirty blues clubs, a new generation is playing.

As I drove, I remembered a dinner in Atlanta a few months before with Koko Taylor. She calls herself the Queen of the Blues and no one disputes it. Over a meal of fried chicken and ham hocks with greens on the side at

Paschal's Restaurant, we talked about Chicago and the blues. Koko is a big woman and onstage her voice growls with authority. But when she is not performing she is quiet, almost demure.

"I moved to Chicago from Memphis in 1953 and I been there ever since," Koko says as she scans the menu. "I was born and raised in Memphis but Chicago is home to me now. But you know what? I'm always glad to go back to Memphis because I have relatives there, lots of nieces and nephews. So I tell folks that when y'all send me to Memphis, you just throwed the rabbit in the briar patch. You know, Memphis is a nice town and I wouldn't mind going back there to live when I retire. But I don't know when that's gonna be, because as long as I'm able to be out singing the blues, that's what I'm gonna be doing.

"Back in Memphis, I wasn't singing the blues as far as recording or performing or anything like that. I was singing blues for my own enjoyment. This was me and my brothers and sisters. See, my three brothers and sisters all grew up singing the blues and singing gospel, too. But the blues was like weekdays. Starting on Monday and going through Saturday we would go to the cotton field. I was raised up on what they called a sharecropper's farm in Bartlett, Tennessee, just outside of Memphis on the rural route. And we would go to the cotton field and sing the blues among ourselves. And on Sundays I would sing with the gospel choir in a little Baptist church. What it amounted to was we sung gospel on Sunday and the blues on Monday.

"They used to always say the blues was the devil's music but I never felt that. I thought the blues was a music that was inspiring and it felt good to me like it still does today. I get the same feeling deep down within me when

I sing the blues, just like I feel when I sing a gospel tune. I can't get into a song until I feel it. Both of 'em are just real good traditional music. The difference is in the words you sing.

"And during those times that I was singing blues in the cotton fields, we had an old Graphanolia—a record player where you don't use electricity, you wind it up with your hand. We would crank it up like you used to crank up cars. During those days I grew up without electricity. I didn't even know what electricity was until I went to the white people's house and washed their clothes and scrubbed their floors and nursed their children.

"When I first got to Chicago, I worked in hotels, worked in laundries, and did domestic work—taking care of people's childrens, all that kind of stuff. I worked all my life," Koko said.

"You understand that when I first went to the clubs in Chicago, I wasn't looking for work singing. I went because me and my husband, Pop, was going out for a good time. And I still loved singing. And a lot of the guys I had been listening to on records ended up right there in Chicago. Like Howlin' Wolf and J. B. Lenoir, Muddy Waters, Sonny Boy Williams. All these people were right there. Right in Chicago. And we would go to these little black clubs on the South Side and the West Side and there they were.

"It was at these clubs that we got acquainted with these guys that were on the records. Let's say, for instance, that Elmore James's band was playing at Sylvio's and me and Pop went there. All the guys were friendly. Now, it wasn't a place where you needed a reservation to get in. It was just a little old black South Side club. You paid a dollar to get in and that's that. Anyway, we got to know all the guys and all the guys got to know me and Pop. I would ask them if I could do a song with them and they would always say yes. Then they'd work with me trying to understand what I wanted to sing or do. So I got to where I would just go and sit in with them. It got to where all the guys knew me all over town. I would frequently sit in with Muddy Waters and all of 'em.

"Sometimes they'd say, 'Here come our girl! Come on! You want to do a tune? Do a couple of tunes!' And it just kept up like that. I was doing it for my own enjoyment. There wasn't no money. And that happened until I was in this club—it was called the Beale Street Club—on a Sunday and they were having a contest where the best band and the best singer would win a prize. They had three prizes. The best singer would get a chicken sandwich. The second prize was a fish sandwich, and the third prize was a hot dog. So I sang that night and Willie Dixon happened to be in the audience.

"Now, you know, Willie Dixon was the man that was in charge of all the artists for Chess Records. And when I finished, Willie Dixon came over and said, 'My God! Where did you come from? I ain't never heard a woman sing the blues like you sing the blues. That's what the world needs today. More women singing the blues. We got plenty of men singing but we don't have no women.' And I said I came from Memphis. Then he asked me, 'Who do you record for?' I didn't even know the meaning of the word. I didn't know what 'record' meant. So he asked me if I'd be interested in going for an audition and then signing a contract. 'I'd like for Leonard Chess and the guys down at Chess Records to hear you,' he said. I told him, yeah. And the next day Willie Dixon carried me down there and Leonard Chess agreed that this is the voice we been looking for and this and that. That was the beginning of my real career.

"Now, during all that, I did record on the Spivey label. But the way that happened, I didn't go in no studio to record. I didn't know I was even recording until it came out. The way that came about, we were in Willie Dixon's basement—me, Sunnyland Slim, Johnny Shines, J. B. Lenoir—just a bunch of guys sitting around going over some tunes. It was like having a party, you know. And everybody was singing their song. This stuff that was re-corded, it wasn't even a song, just words I put together. So I sung these two tunes and I never thought no more about it. When I heard from them tunes again they was on this recording. We're talking seven or eight years later.

"Now, the first song I recorded for Willie Dixon on Chess was, 'I Got What it Takes.' During those years, I got to know people like Muddy Waters and Howlin' Wolf real well. The Wolf was a hard worker. A very sincere guy about his music. He was also the type of musician that if his band didn't play the tunes right and do like they were supposed to have done, he just might grab 'em in the collar. But he was a very nice man to me. I recorded 'Evil' and 'Spoonful,' but those weren't really Howlin' Wolf's songs. They were Willie Dixon tunes and me and the Wolf both did 'em. But Muddy! Oh, Muddy! That was like my brother. Yeah, I spent a lot of time with him. I worked with him a lot more times than fingers and toes. 'Til he passed away.

"I made a whole bunch of them little bitty records for Chess. You know, the little forty-five's. And people never knew anything about them because I would record them for Chess and they'd put them on the shelf and they'd collect dust. In those days, during the daytime, I was doing domestic work in a Chicago suburb. I would work for different rich families up there and I was scrubbing floors, doing domestic work—what I was used to doing in the South. I really didn't get my opportunities in the clubs because I was just working on weekends.

"When I stopped that work was when 'Wang Dang Doodle' hit the chart and they told me it done sold a million copies. 'Wang Dang Doodle' was one of those tunes that looked like it caught on by itself. They played that tune one time on WVON, a black radio station in Chicago, and it just caught fire. So that's when I got my band, The Blues Machine, together and started touring with Jimmy Reed, Otis Redding, Tina Turner, a bunch of everybody. See, back then Tina wasn't no bigger a star than me. We all be tryin' to make it.

"There's been some good times but there have been bad times too when it's been disgusting. Believe me when I tell you it's not peaches and cream, even today. Blues people like myself, we get less recognition, we get less airplay, less money for working and it's really hard. And people ask me why isn't there more women, other girls, singing the blues. Well, this is the reason why. Most girls who are out there singing would rather be doing the type of music where they're gonna get more recognition, more money, more everything.

"You take Whitney Houston, Aretha Franklin, Tina Turner, and all those people. They know how to sing the blues. Tina can sing the blues good as I can. But she's in a field where you turn on the radio, you're gonna hear something by Tina Turner. You gonna hear something by Whitney Houston. But you may never hear anything by Koko Taylor on that same station. That's how it is. That's the difference in how people treat blues musicians and people in pop or rock music. You know, I used to think about crossing over, but blues is what I want to do. And to do what I'm doing, you gotta want to do it. Because you get to thinking how you could make more money doing something else. So you got to be real strong to stick with it.

"The younger people, you just don't find 'em today who want to sing the blues. They use the name *blues*, but when you listen to 'em, they're really doing rock or something else and they never really touch the bottom of the barrel."

The waitress brings Koko her Coke, no ice. She takes a sip and then continues.

"Now, when I first came to Chicago, Muddy Waters was my number-one idol. When I started singing professionally, the other girls singing in Chicago were, let's see, there was Lucille Spann, Otis Spann's wife. Otis was Muddy's piano player. But Lucille was just singing local, she wasn't into recording or anything like that. And Etta James was singing. She was with Chess Records, the same company I started out with. But it wasn't too many women that was singing the blues. Back then it was mostly men they were pushing, and it's the same today.

"The difference between working for Chess back then and working for Alligator—that's who I record for now —is almost as much difference as between night and day for me. Of course Chess is where Muddy and Howlin' Wolf and Sonny Boy and all them recorded. So it was the place to be. But when I was with Chess, the number-one thing was that every song I recorded was tunes that somebody would write and then come to me and say, 'I want you to do this.' It made no difference whether I liked it or whether I could do it—they didn't ask you that. I didn't have no say-so over recording certain tunes.

"But with Bruce Iglauer at Alligator, it's different. Bruce and I get together and we'll talk about tunes, we'll suggest tunes and we'll come up with ideas. I tell him about my ideas and he tells me about his. And he'll say to me, 'Well, you know, Koko, I got this song here and I want you to take a listen to it, see what you think about it. Do you think it's a good tune?' I mean, he would just bring it to me as a suggestion, same as I go to him with suggestions. That's how we get together on what to record. With Chess, I never had that opportunity. They said, 'Your job is to sing, I'll take care of the rest.' It was just like doing a job with Chess. Now I enjoy it."

The food arrived.

"This is too much," Koko said, surveying the plate. "I can't eat all of this. I got a show to do. After the show, well, I could eat it. But . . ."

Between bites of ham hocks and fried chicken, she talked about today's blues audience.

"It's a funny thing, but blacks do not support blacks. I mean, it's the truth. I'm not just saying it. I would love to say that blacks support me. But they don't. Just like if you go to the club where I'm at now, you'll see two hundred whites and you could count the blacks on one hand. The white people, that's who's promoting the blues, that's who likes the blues today. And, let's face it, we have to go with who supports us. It's not like it was when I came to Chicago, things have changed. Black people just do not listen to the blues. Everywhere I work is like ninety-five percent white clubs, white audiences.

"Right now they got white clubs on Chicago's North Side and you can go to a different club seven nights a week. Back in those early days, Baby, and we're talking twenty years ago, the only way somebody black got to the North Side was if they had a domestic job up there. That's why I started singing in the little clubs on the South Side. There're a few clubs left playing blues on the South Side, but they're not hittin' on nothin'. All of the bands go to the North Side now because they can make a few bucks more and they can get regular work. You take the black clubs right now, like the Checkerboard. The only thing happening, the best thing happening, is Friday and Saturday night. Just like it was twenty years ago. On the North Side, they got a little club on Halsted and they got three hundred people packed in there on Monday night. You go to the Checkerboard on Monday night and you throw a brick and you don't hit nobody."

Koko faded from my mind when I hit the outskirts of Chicago. As I inched down the Eisenhower Parkway toward the turn to Lakeshore Drive, I decided the first person in town I needed to see was Bruce Iglauer, the man who's keeping the Chicago blues on record.

Alligator Records, the company that records the best of America's contemporary blues, is on Chicago's North Side in a narrow, three-story building across from a supermarket and down the street from a deli. There is no sign on the front, no stuffed alligator peering from behind the dirty window on the ground floor. Iglauer, Alligator's president and founder, is upstairs in his office. A handful of employees move back and forth from their desks to the storage area on the first floor. Two people are hand-packing compact discs. There are posters on the walls from past festivals and posters celebrating Alligator's stable of musicians. But the place still has the atmosphere of a political headquarters, a place without permanence, where frenzied activity might all be for naught. But, like political volunteers, the people work with zeal and dedication.

Iglauer bounds down the front stairs, dressed in jeans and a T-shirt from a rival record company. He is in his late thirties, bearded, slim, and bespectacled, with a full head of black curly hair. An old girlfriend used to call him Little Alligator because he tapped his teeth in time to music he was hearing.

We're scheduled to meet Johnny Littlejohn, a Chicago slide-guitarist who's leaving on a two-week Scandinavian tour. "It's a forty-five-minute drive to the airport," Iglauer says, "and we've got fifteen minutes to get there." We hop into his car and drive down Peterson Avenue and then inch our way through the dense ribbons of traffic.

Bruce Iglauer is a native of Cincinnati who went to college in Appleton, Wisconsin, got caught up in the folk-music revival and gradually drifted from Peter, Paul, and Mary to Sleepy John Estes and Bukka White. "I didn't really know much about the blues until 1966 or 1967," he says as he lights a cigar. "I was playing in a lot of little jug bands and stuff—and I got into the blues by reading liner notes on albums by people like Geoff Muldaur." He guns the engine and moves into the left lane, around a car, and then back to the right. "I came to Chicago the year I graduated from college and went to work for Bob Koester at Delmark Records. I was a shipping clerk, the only Delmark employee except Bob. He was, like, my idol. Just before I went to work for him he had recorded wonderful albums by Junior Wells, Magic Sam, and Roosevelt Sykes." Iglauer slams on his brakes.

As we turn onto the Kennedy Expressway, traffic is backed up in all four lanes. "In 1971 I recorded Hound

Dog Taylor and took a three-week leave of absence to promote it. After that, about half the calls Delmark got were for Hound Dog Taylor bookings, so in June of seventy-two, Bob sat me down and said, 'Make up your mind. It's one thing or another.' He was right, you know. In the beginning, I really didn't think Alligator was going to be a full-time job."

The car in front of us begins to creep forward. Iglauer's cigar goes out, he relights it, edges his way into the right lane, and shifts into third gear. "Most of my audience is white," he says. "The label was originally designed to sell records to me. I was my target market—male, reasonably well educated, middle class, and a sixties-type guy interested in culture outside what I'd grown up knowing. We've made some intrusions into the black market, but a black audience is based almost entirely on airplay, and that's not always easy to come by. To get airplay, you need to spend a lot of promotional money I don't have."

Traffic is whizzing by now and Iglauer shifts into fourth. "I've never really directed this business toward hits," he says, "so it's not surprising we've never had any. I stay in business by making records that break even at five thousand copies. And I don't take anything out of print, ever. See, we don't make records that are going to sound different. If our records sound old-fashioned now, they're not going to sound any more old-fashioned in ten years. The blues changes and evolves very slowly. But that doesn't bother me. You know, a great steak is a great steak, and if you've tasted one, it doesn't mean you don't want to taste another."

"But with such a limited audience," I ask as he eases into the left lane, "how do blues musicians stay in the business? How do they make a living?"

"In a lot of ways," he says as he changes lanes again, "blues musicians aren't in the music business. The vast majority of people who play the blues in Chicago have day jobs. They play basically for fun. Look at the people I'm sending to Europe today. Until he had a heart attack not long ago, Johnny Littlejohn ran a garage. Aaron Burton just quit his job as a gardener for the Chicago Parks Department. And it's true of other blues musicians, too. Son Seals worked for a while as a country-club chef, Koko Taylor worked as a hotel maid to bankroll her career. Blues musicians can make modest money but it would be a big deal to be making as much as a middle-weight country act. All in all, blues musicians can do OK and live a middle-class life if they're willing to go out and drive 500 to 1,000 miles a day, work 150 nights a year, and lug their own amplifiers around."

Iglauer cuts into the right lane and makes the exit to O'Hare. "Blues is music with a lack of pretension. It's working-class music for people who are comfortable with themselves and don't have a lot to prove, who aren't ashamed to be working-class or show a little emotion. It takes pride in not being music for the Michael Jackson set." Traffic is slowing again and Iglauer glances at his watch. It's only a few minutes before the Lufthansa flight takes off. "You know, the blues is so intensely emotional and so raw, it's never gonna be hugely popular. It can't be. Teenagers buy most of the records and the blues is grown-up music."

At the airport, Iglauer squeezes into an illegal parking space, grabs a box of promotional records, and runs toward the international gate, dodging women in saris and men in barrets. Johnny Littlejohn is at the bar, drinking a screwdriver, waiting for his flight to be called.

"Hey, what's the matter Bruce?" Littlejohn says as Iglauer arrives breathlessly. "You think we can't get on the plane by ourselves?" Littlejohn is a massive middle-aged black man who migrated to Chicago from Jackson, Mississippi, in the 1950s. He seems no more excited about a two-week trip to Stockholm than he would be about a quick flight to Milwaukee.

"It ain't my first trip to Europe," he tells me. "I been all over. Oh, man, those people in Europe go crazy, those folks are wild for the blues. These people here? They ain't into blues. Oh, you got a few white youngsters here that are into the blues, they love the blues. But not like in foreign countries. People here think the blues is the lowest thing you can do. But when I played in Tokyo, those people went plumb crazy over there. Anywhere out of this country, you get a lot of action.

"I'm from Jackson, Mississippi. Oh, shit, man. I came up here thirty-seven or thirty-eight years ago. I came for a better living. Because I could work for more money than I was gettin' in Mississippi. I couldn't live on forty cents a day. I picked cotton, I chopped cotton, I drove bulldozer, I drove tractors, I drove tractor-trailers. I did it all. And it's sure a better living up here. It's much, much better and I ain't thought once about going back that way.

"I went back to visit my mother not long ago and there is a big difference in the South now. But it was a madhouse forty years ago. Even a poor white man would have to try to get away from there because that part of the country is for rich people only. I didn't play for nothing but whites when I was down there. But no one could go up to the bandstand and mess with the musicians. I was on the radio every day, too. On WLKJ. So everywhere I played I would have that sort of advance word. The radio would make peoples want to come out and see you.

"Even back in Jackson I played the same kind of music that I play now. I originated with the blues and that's what I'm gonna play. I'll stick to it.

"If I told you where I learned to play, you wouldn't believe me. It was a guy grew up with my mother and father and he used to play at house parties," Littlejohn said, "and he was the first man I ever seen play a guitar. I had heard a lot of guitars on the radio and on records, but I never seen one till then. 'Cause back then, you didn't have no TV. The man was Henry Martin. He played one of them old round guitars, them Gene Autry kind. I watched him, and he was moving his fingers so fast I didn't know which route to take. But what happened, the sound got in my head—and pretty soon, I knew how the sound went. And I kept it in my head until I learned how to do it. Now this wasn't no electric guitar I started out on— because the guitar I was playing, my father won in a crap game and brought it home. And he set it up in the corner, you know. I started messing with it. I slipped around and messed with it while he was gone and I got where I could get a little sound out of it. My mother used to say, 'You better not let your daddy catch you with that box.' I played a little electric guitar down there even though I learned on that old Gene Autry. I switched to electric because I liked that sound best. When that stereo Gibson came out, oh, that had a sound. I just got hooked on it and I been playing a Gibson ever since.

"Back in Mississippi, I used to listen to Jimmy Wakely, Tex Ritter, all those guys you could see on the screen. And I used to listen to Howlin' Wolf, B. B. King, Muddy Waters, Elmore James—all those guys. I got me a little band together and we used to play at fish fries, house parties, and all that. Then when I come to Chicago, I worked some with the John Brim Band, with Jimmy Reed, and toured some with Howlin' Wolf. And now . . . here I am!"

There is a call for the Lufthansa flight. Littlejohn finishes his drink, slaps Bruce on the back, and heads off for Scandinavia. Bruce and I drive back into town and agree to meet at an Indian restaurant near his office for dinner.

That night, over drinks and curry, Bruce talked about the blues in Chicago, about racism, and about his musical philosophy.

"I remember years ago, just after I'd moved to Chicago, I had somebody crashing with me who was a Yale student. His name was Jay Sullivan and I remember he went out to the West Side to a club Eddie Shaw was running on West Madison. Sometimes, he'd kind of slip in because he was a blues freak. See, he was under age for drinking.

"In this case it was a Blue Monday, that's sort of a jam session around here. And they had a good Blue Monday at Eddie Shaw's place. The place was a little—you know, just a tavern—a bar down one side, a few booths, and they put the band at the end. It wasn't a show room in any way. Anyway, Jay was standing outside on the street leaning against the car. And a little ways down there were a couple of guys shooting dice. All of a sudden, an unmarked car pulls up and a couple of people jump out and line up the guys who are shooting dice against the car, frisk them, and put them in the backseat. Then they turn to Jay and say, 'Let's see your ID.' He claims that he said, 'If you're police officers, can I please see your badges?' At which point they beat the hell out of him with one of those big flashlights. He came back to my apartment about three in the morning, all covered with blood. Because after they beat him, they threw him in jail. Turns out they *were* cops. That's what it used to be like going to blues bars on public transportation. He was on the bus.

"But then I remember being stopped on the West Side in the Winter of seventy-one. I was stopped simply for being white. The police pulled me over and wanted to know what I was doing on the West Side, why I was in that neighborhood. It was a black cop and he was very concerned. I think he thought I was involved in a drug or sexual experience. But, you know that kind of thing was a long time ago. All my dramatic experiences in the ghetto have been at least ten years ago. I've had nothing happen to me for ages."

Bruce ate a little curry and washed it down with some wine. We began talking about why people listen to the blues.

"I feel like blues is music that allows people to express themselves with the music in a way they wouldn't do otherwise. It's as though those blues musicians are saying what you need to say to yourself. I keep telling people that if it weren't for the blues, I'd be a crazy person. I suspect I *am* a crazy person, but it's easier to hide it in the music. I need the music almost every day. You know, Louis Armstrong used to have hot chocolate at night and a little release in the morning. Well, it's necessary for me to have a little release every morning too. And sometimes, in addition to other kinds of releases, that's the blues. You listen to the blues to get rid of the blues. Echoing your feeling to purge your feeling makes some sense. To me, the blues is communal music. You know that country song, 'Hank Williams, You Wrote My Life'? The blues is like that all the time. One of the things that happens is that you sit there and listen to the song and suddenly realize the singer is singing about things that happen to you. You're not alone.

And then you look around and see two or three other people who are also saying, 'That's about me.' That's why I call the blues a communal music. You know, when you got a hole in your soul, it doesn't matter how much money you got."

Over dessert, Iglauer began talking about his idea of recording. "I don't want anyone recording for me who's disappointed with the results. I want people who feel they've achieved their maximum potential at this point in their career. It's very upsetting to me when people say, 'I'd have been a big star by now if I'd been with a big label.' People say that sometimes. Not too often, but it's said. And it hurts. I don't want to share anyone. If I record somebody, I really want to feel like I can record them again without somebody else getting in the way.

"I guess in terms of a small label, we're kinda like the old Prestige jazz label. But, then, I'd kinda like to make the comparison with Blue Note. They ended up with about a hundred-fifty albums. If anyone wanted to compare me with Alfred Lion in the quality of my music or the way I treated my musicians, I'd be complimented.

Over coffee, the conversation drifted to changes in the blues and the way the music was passed along from generation to generation.

"How else do you learn music except by hearing other people play? How else do young people learn except by old people teaching them? We're talking here about a hundred years, five generations between when somebody gets yanked out of Africa and when somebody was dragged into some hotel room to make a record. I mean, imagine five generations between 1350 and 1450. How much did music change then? Not much. But from 1887 to 1987? Big change. And the change all started in 1920. So we're down to fifty-seven years versus the rest of human history. We're talking about something unprecedented."

We talked for a while about people who record for him, about Son Seals, about Albert Collins and Koko Taylor and Johnny Winter. If I really wanted to know about blues recording in Chicago, he said, I should talk to Bob Koester, the owner of the Jazz Record Mart and Delmark Records. Since Chess Records closed, he said, Koester had been recording blues longer than anyone in town. Fine, I said, I'll see him tomorrow. But what I wanted to find was the ultimate Chicago bluesman. I knew the big names were dead, and I knew the scene had changed. But there had to be somebody who was an anachronism, someone who was still like the good old days.

"Well, if anybody was ever a bluesman," Bruce said, "I guess it would be Magic Slim."

He was playing that night at the Checkerboard Lounge. I decided to go. Magic Slim's real name is Morris Holt, although probably nobody has called him that for years. After he moved to Chicago from Granada, Mississippi, in the late 1940s, he worked with a Mississippi school classmate, Samuel Maghett, aka Magic Sam. It was Sam who first called him Magic Slim, and it was Sam's legacy he was trying to carry on.

I drove across town to the fabled South Side, where most people say the Chicago blues was born. The famous clubs—Theresa's, Sylvio's, Jake's Tavern, and Pepper's— are gone now. I passed the giant high-rise ghetto housing projects, turned onto Forty-third Street, and parked in front of God's House for All Nations. Magic Slim is next door, wearing a huge black cowboy hat and standing in front of a red-and-white-checked storefront, smoking a cigarette and drinking Wild Turkey. Slim flips his cigarette into the street, moves his six-foot-five-inch hulk inside, and steps on to a stage lit with one bare light bulb hanging down from a cord and swinging precariously close to his head. *He may be magic*, I think as I look at him, *but he's damn sure not slim.*

"Everybody wanna hear the blues, say yeah," he shouts.

"*Yeah,*" screams the audience, and Magic Slim picks up his guitar and begins to play. A lone dancer—young, acrobatic, and a little crazy—swoons and dives in front of the stage. He is like a whirling dervish, twisting and writhing with the music until he glides away from the stage, slumps against a back wall, and passes out.

As Magic Slim plays, I tap my foot, then pound the table, and finally, shout along with everyone else in the Checkerboard: "Hey! Hey! The blues is all right! Hey! Hey! The blues is all right!"

The set ended and Slim walked toward the bar. By the time I edged my way out of the room, he was gone. No problem, I figured. He'd be appearing tomorrow night at the Cuddle Inn Cuddle Den on South Ashland. I could catch him there. I got in the car and headed for home. Tomorrow I'd get a history lesson from Bob Koester, then catch Slim again.

Koester's Delmark records is on Lincoln Avenue in a run-down storefront. He was inside, sorting through a batch of sixteen-millimeter movies. It seems that in addition to running what may be the nation's biggest jazz and blues record store and managing his own record label, Koester also collects movies.

He is a short, stocky man with a full, white beard and as he files the movies, he talks about his beginnings in music.

"I grew up in Wichita, Kansas. When you're sitting out there in the 1940s like I was, you're pretty much isolated, particularly if you're a nonjock. I had polio in the sixth grade. And you can find solace by going into a different kind of music. So I got interested in jazz. I was awfully tired of some of the shitty pop tunes that were popular in the 1940s. I remember hearing records with Count Basie and Fats Waller and I was just sort of drawn to jazz, but particularly to boogie-woogie and blues. Boogie-woogie was my first choice, but, still, I was into blues. But I got so I liked any kind of black music. There was one half-hour gospel show from the local church—'And now KFH brings you the music and sounds of a great people from the little white-washed, weatherbeaten church on Fourteenth Street,'—or something like that. In a way it was like the radio station was saying, 'Sorry, folks, but we gotta let the Negroes have a little space here.' But it was a great show.

"And there was a record store there that had a lot of blues and jazz that came in with their hillbilly stuff—Memphis Minnie, Big Bill Broonzy, people like that. Now Bruce and some others will disagree with me on this, but I see blues and jazz as just part of the same system. Oh, it has its little separate life, but there's so much feedback back and forth between blues and jazz that I regard blues as not really a separate music form at all.

"My parents decided I had to go to a Catholic school, so I went to St. Louis. I wanted to be a cameraman, that's what started this movie collection, and I decided that if I went to school in either New Orleans or Chicago, I'd get seduced by the music away from my studies. It never occurred to me that all the great bands would be coming through St. Louis, so I got seduced anyway. And I never finished college—and ended up in the record business. I'd just pick up any record I thought I could trade and try to sell it. I had a walk-up store and I specialized in Dixieland. I also started making records in St. Louis—blues, a Dixieland band, and even one bop group. I figured recording Speckled Red and Big Joe Williams was a good move because no one else was doing that. At that time, the only blues being recorded was in the Folkways catalogue.

"I moved to Chicago in August of fifty-eight. That was just after Chess started recording blues artists. But if I carefully phrase it, I can say Delmark was the first label to take a working electric Chicago blues band into the studio for the purpose of recording an LP. The stuff Chess was doing was mostly forty-fives. They had that album, *Muddy Waters at Newport*, but that wasn't made in a studio—so I really felt like we were taking a chance. My first record in Chicago was Junior Wells and 'Hoodoo Man.' It's been a big seller ever since," Koester said.

"After Junior Wells, the smart thing would have been to go out and record everything I could get my hands on. But instead I decided to record a jazz festival that was a commercial failure. Now, the penalty for being in on the ground floor with the blues is that you're in too soon. You don't know what you've got. When there's so much of something around, when it's in the air and on every street corner for free, you don't know what you've got. How can you respect something they're giving away for free on a street corner? It was such a pioneering thing—you just can't realize how obscure these guys were. But, a lot of the fun's gone out of it. There are damn few mysteries left in the blues.

"I think there's been a basic change in Chicago blues. It's not so much a folk idiom anymore. Now, of course, there are some who say that as soon as the musicians plugged into that electric amp, it wasn't a folk idiom. But I think that's bullshit. What I mean is that since the blues isn't really a folk idiom anymore, it's just one of many career choices open to young blacks. Some of these young guys who're playing blues now, I wouldn't be surprised if they moved on into soul music or jazz. The truth is, if I want to hear someone who's as self-conscious about their playing as some of these people are, I'm gonna be much more interested in jazz.

"You know, when you talk about the blues, you've got to realize this: I can think of about six guys, and if they passed away we'd have a problem. This new interest in the blues, I think it stems from two things—the black pride movement and the chamber of commerce attitude down South. First it happened in New Orleans. Then in Memphis and in Mississippi. Who would have ever predicted that they'd be studying the blues in academia in Mississippi?

"I keep going out trying to find the next superstar. But now these guys play at North Side bars like B.L.U.E.S. and they don't have to play ghetto bars anymore. That's what's making it less of a folk art. Before, you seldom saw a black band on the North Side. In the sixties, the big North Side blues bar was Big John's. And if they couldn't get a white band in there, maybe they'd hire Muddy. They'd condescend to bring in Muddy Waters and Junior Wells. Now when they did that, when they brought black performers to the North Side, it was very valuable. But it was only an occasional thing. Back then, Muddy was still the house band at Pepper's Lounge, and Howlin' Wolf would have been at Sylvio's most of the time in those days. The ghetto bar was the base of operations. It was sort of a paid rehearsal. You played there week in and week out unless something better came along. And that was the understanding. With a better gig, they could leave with one hour's notice," Koester said.

"The most fabulous scene was when Muddy and Wolf both played at Sylvio's. And Magic Sam and Shaky Jake would play at intermission. Sylvio was a nice old Italian man. He did OK in the ghetto and he probably wasn't exploiting the people that much. Unfortunately, he got burned out during the West Side riots. Now, among the club owners, there were a lot of bastards out there, but Sylvio was a guy who liked the music. Hell, Elmore James was the bartender there sometimes. Sylvio used to say, 'I gotta hire two bands just to make sure I got one good one.'

"But it's so different now. There's not a club that has a house band, where the musicians leave their instruments there overnight. It's all a calendar thing—a different band every night. I guess that's good in a way, because it gives work to more people.

"Some people say Bruce and Alligator records are the new Chess of Chicago. But Chess is gone. And it's a completely different business now. Chess was hot when forty-fives were selling. Now it's all LPs. And that's what Bruce records. But the market's so different. Blues doesn't get airplay. Me? I'm much less commercial than Bruce. I record more doomed records than he does, things that don't have an obvious market. I don't mean to imply I'm a saint or anything. I may just be stupid. Who knows?"

Certainly not me. I left Koester to his films, got back in the car, and drove over to Gerry's Kitchen in West North Avenue for some turnip greens and a chance to talk with James Cotton. Like Koko Taylor, Cotton followed the blues route from Memphis to Chicago and, like Koko Taylor, he's on the road most of the year. But today he was in Chicago.

I parked on North, just down the street from the restaurant, and walked in. Once the area around the now-defunct "Old Town," North Avenue seemed to be a pleasant mixture of small shops and residences, an amalgam of income levels and interests. Gerry's is a neighborhood restaurant specializing in Southern cooking. This far north of the Mason-Dixon line it's called "soul food," and apparently is thought to be food for blacks—something of an exotic experience for anyone not born in either the ghetto or a sharecropper's shack. But I know better.

Inside Gerry's, I ordered pork chops and greens and waited for Cotton. It didn't take long. He sat down, ordered vegetable soup, and began talking about his career, which began when he was ten years old.

"Well, my uncle had quite a bit to do with me leaving home when I was ten," Cotton says. "He partially raised me, you see. I was his pick out of nine kids. He didn't play no instrument or nothing—he just liked the blues. You know, one of those kind of guys who liked to go out and party. And when he found out I was trying to play music, he helped me.

"My family wasn't able to buy me any other instrument. They couldn't afford a drum, guitar, or anything like that. So they got me an American Ace harmonica. It cost fifteen cents.

"Really, it was Sonny Boy Williamson who took me

away. See, I drove a tractor every day on the farm. When Sonny Boy finally heard me play, we were sitting on the porch where we got paid off every week. I made thirty-six dollars for driving the tractor for two weeks, and while we were sitting on the porch and I was playing the harmonica, I made forty-six dollars. He said, 'It's time to go.'

"So I went to Helena, Arkansas, and was on the *King Biscuit Hour*. The first time I ever heard a band it was Sonny Boy's band. I was used to people playing a guitar or blowing a jug, stuff like that, but Sonny Boy's Band was something new."

I asked Cotton about all the Sonny Boy legends, about whether he was as mean as people said he was.

"He was getting there," he said. "He was kinda mysterious, he was that. Well, anyway, we started out in Helena and ended up in West Memphis, Arkansas. Off and on, I was with him for six years. Then he left town and gave me his band. See, he and his wife, Mattie Williams, separated and she moved to Milwaukee. I guess he couldn't take it no longer and he said, 'See ya later.' The band stayed together only about six months. I wasn't but fifteen years old. Maybe that's why we didn't stay together long. Then I worked as an iceman, a grocery boy, a short-order cook—and was a bum. It was all black where I was. Then I got a radio-station gig at Station KWEM in West Memphis and that helped us out a lot. Not too long after I went on the air I cut a record, 'Straighten Up, Baby' and 'Cotton Crop Blues.' It was on the Sun label. I got along pretty good with Sam Phillips, who ran Sun, but nothing much changed after the record. Never did get paid for it or nothing. That was the name of the game then—you do the work and everybody else gets the money.

"In 1954, I moved to Chicago. The music up here was

more professional. People up here had been out in it for a while. I went to work in Muddy Water's band. I guess I was the third or fourth harmonica player Muddy had. Let's see, there was Little Walter, Junior Wells, and then me. I came in behind Junior Wells. It was pretty difficult because Walter had already made all those recordings with Muddy and had developed a new style. I still say Little Walter is the world's greatest blues harmonica player. Nothing against Sonny Boy, you know, I like him too. But Sonny Boy played more country.

"The audience for the blues has modernized just like anything else. Entertainers tried to clean it up and bring it uptown. When I came up here, there wasn't any blues on the North Side. From my experience, a lot of people think blues is sad and lonely, but it doesn't have to be like that. I know how to play that way, but I know how to get up and go, too. 'Course, another problem is you don't get much exposure on the radio so people can't find out about the music. It's gettin' a little better now, I guess, but it seems like it's slow in coming and I'm gettin' tired of waitin'.

"I think the blues has changed a lot since I first heard it. Back then it was people like John Lee Hooker, Muddy Waters, and Lightnin' Hopkins. Now everybody's trying to modernize it and get it to happen. The next generation that'll come along to play it, I hear some of these cats and I can't hardly tell it from rock 'n' roll.

"Blues ain't like what Mamma and Daddy heard. But people are afraid to take a chance on it. And the record companies and the radio stations are like that too, I guess," Cotton said.

"You know, they say Chicago has the blues, but it's not Chicago. It's the people who came up here that had the blues. It's still more people in Chicago from Mississippi than there is in Jackson, the state capital. See, this was the next stop where you could find work. Up here, you got a chance to express what you'd learned. Down there, you'd get a job maybe once a week. And that was it. Here, you could work every night.

"But I don't know. I don't know. You look for the blues in a record store, it's just one little rack. Everything else's rock 'n' roll and that shit's all the same beat to me."

Cotton sipped his soup and thought about Mississippi.

"You know, I ain't been on Nelson Street since I played with Willie Love there when I was a kid. We used to play a place called the Silver Dollar Café. It was right on Nelson Street. They even wrote a song about it. Let's see, it was, 'If you ever go to Greenville, please go down on Nelson Street. You'll laugh and have a lot of fun with nearly every-one you meet.' Willie Love did that, called it 'Nelson Street Blues.' You got me to remembering, now. The first record I played on was with Howlin' Wolf. We were doing a song called 'How Many More Years?' and the flip side was 'Morning and Midnight.' And we played this club at 508 Beale Street called the Hippodrome. I just had one harp to tune up the band and those guys they said, 'Ah, get out of here.' Then Howlin' Wolf told 'em to cool it. 'That's where the hit records come from,' he said. The band didn't say nothing else.

"But I been everywhere. I remember the last time we was in Kansas City we left the town runnin'—and we weren't even playing there. We just stopped to get some-thing to eat. We were at this place and our bass player went walking out the door with this girl. He wasn't gone more than three seconds and all of a sudden there was gunshots. We figured her old man was out there. But it turned out there was a dice game going on between the cars. Somebody in the game got mad at somebody else and started shooting. Now, this girl our bass player walked outside with was pretty plastered. She walked back into the joint when the shooting started and just fell on the floor. It had nothing to do with him, you understand. A couple of guys in the band were still out in the van. When the shooting started, they just dove on the floor. We paid and left. That was our last trip to Kansas City.

"The thing is, when you get used to being on the road, used to working at night, you can't sleep like ordinary people do. I was up shaving at two this morning. Then I was up again at six.

"You know, usually, when I come home, it takes a few days for me to calm down and adjust. So when I get back I go out to a few clubs, things like that. I remember one time, two or three years ago, it was my wife's birthday and I had to get her a present. So I sent her some flowers. That messed me up bad. I came back off the road and started to go out like I used to do and she wouldn't let me. My wife turned around and fell in love with me again. It took about two weeks before I could go out without getting in trouble at home. No more flowers."

Cotton finished his soup, sighed, leaned back and lit a cigarette.

"You know, I come up here to Chicago broke, and I'm still broke. I guess that's one reason I got the blues. I'll never get rich. I don't care about that. I just want to be comfortable. In a way, I'd like to move back to West Memphis. Seems like the blues have more meaning in the South. And so I go there every chance I get. But Chicago, that's where it's happening. That's where you find the work."

I left Cotton, paid the check, and walked toward my car. There was something wrong. I couldn't tell what it was at first, but as I got closer, I knew. The passenger window had been smashed.

A black woman walked out onto her front stoop. "That your car?" she asked.

"Sure is."

"I seen the kid that done it. We was out here, just got home, me and my friend, and she says, 'Look at the car. There's a man just sittin' in it on the passenger side. That ain't right.' Then I notice the window's broke. And I say, 'Man, he ain't just sittin' in it—he done broke out the window. Look. That ain't his car.' And he hears us and gets out and starts runnin' down the street. He wasn't black, though. He was, what you call it?—Spanish—Hispanic."

I thanked the woman and asked her to go in and call the police. A few minutes later a cop arrived and looked at the window and the out-of-state license plate.

"Welcome to the city," he said.

The cop filled out the forms I'd need to make an insurance claim and I drove off in search of a place that sold car windows. The wind whipped through the car and my hands felt frozen as I negotiated through the traffic. Up until then, I thought the Chicago blues was just a song.

Since I had a couple of hours to kill while the car was being fixed, I decided to call up Purvis Spann. He's a disc jockey and part-owner of WVON, a radio station that used to play a lot of blues. For years people said that Spann could make a musician a star. WVON is a strange radio station. From ten at night until one in the afternoon it's black-owned and plays black programming. The rest of the time, it's a Polish station. You could be listening to the blues for lunch and all of a sudden it would change into a polka.

When I get to Spann, he tells me he doesn't play blues anymore. It's a gospel/talk/inspirational station now.

"There are a number of reasons we don't play the blues, a number of reasons." He speaks in slow, deliberate, mellow tones. "One of the reasons is that the programmers here and at most black radio stations are young individuals. And they don't relate to blues. So the blues don't get played. People don't hear it. So they think they don't like it. If it got played, people would like it and relate to it and they'd be more blues."

He said he played blues records until about three months before when the station switched to the talk format.

"We don't have a lot of time on the air, so we can't be flexible. But, you know, it's the people on the North Side, basically the young whites, who are keeping the blues alive. A few years ago, they acquired a taste for the blues during the time the late Muddy Waters was living. Since that time they have supported it—they will come out for concerts. Blues is basically supported by two elements—young whites and old blacks. And that's just the way it is.

"And since it's supported by those two groups, the young black programmer, who is oriented to music young blacks would like to hear, he is not going to play music for old blacks. He's going to play the young entertainers, the Michael Jacksons and others who fit in that category. So therefore, the blues don't get played as much in black radio. You'll probably hear more blues on white stations.

"I would like to play the blues. But I own thirty-six percent of this radio station. I don't own fifty-one percent. And those who own fifty-one percent say we're going pretty good with an inspirational format. So I only play inspiration music, between the talk, just to keep the flow going. The thing is, this station is making money with the talk, and that's the bottom line in any business.

"Of course, with the blues, you've got to realize it's not the same as it was in years past. A lot of the major performers died. And only a very few have come on the scene to take their place. The void is not being filled by young musicians," Spann said.

"The blues is a good music. The lyrics are usually very strong. Last year and the year before we gave a blues festival in Chicago and ended up with forty thousand to fifty thousand who came out just to hear the music.

"You know, I also own a radio station in Memphis. And my programming was urban contemporary. And I just lost my ratings. I just got beat to death by these hundred-thousand-watt FM giants. So I changed my programming to all blues and my ratings just shot up. So the blues is not dead, it's just laying dormant. But this is a temporary thing. Pretty soon someone will see the void and start playing the blues on Chicago radio again."

After the car was fixed I drove over to the South Side to see Magic Slim again. Tonight he was playing at the Cuddle Inn on South Ashland. It's just a neighborhood bar, but once a week they have live blues. Usually, it's Magic Slim. The bar has an unimposing sign out front advertising OLD STYLE BEER and proclaiming itself THE CUDDLE INN CUDDLE DEN. The front room was almost empty and the few people at the bar turned and stared at me when I came in.

"Magic Slim playing here?" I asked.

"Later," one woman said, and then turned back to her beer. I left and drove around for a while. Most of the streets were empty and the few bars I passed seemed quiet. In the 1950s, Ashland was the home of Club Zanzibar and Vi's Lounge, but those two blues bars have been gone for years.

I circled the block and went back to the Cuddle Inn. There were more people inside now and I was told the music was in the back room. This joint was no Checkerboard. There were tablecloths on the table, the waitresses were pretty and attentive. The crowd was mostly middle-aged, out for a night on the neighborhood, probably waiting to cuddle. After a few minutes of records, Magic Slim and his Teardrops came in, tuned up, and started playing. The music was different from what I'd heard at the Checkerboard, where it pounded the audience into a frenzy. There was still Magic Slim's wailing guitar, but the tempo was a little slower and the singing a little more mellow. At the Cuddle Inn, people talked back to Slim while he played, shouted requests, and offered criticism.

"Not as good as last week, man. Pick it up," one man shouted.

"Yeah, I know about you last week," Slim said. "Don't forget, I was here."

On the wall there was a four-foot-square poster. It showed a bluesman in a big cowboy hat—obviously Magic Slim—riding a horse. Across his lap was a naked white woman. She was face down. The bluesman's hand was raised above her rear end. HEY! HEY! THE BLUES IS ALL RIGHT! was written below the picture.

When the set ended, I walked up to the bar and introduced myself to Slim.

"Got time to talk?" I asked.

"Well, yeah," he said, and then hesitated. "Look, this place ain't really right for us talking, though, you know what I mean? It's too noisy. You come over to the Checkerboard tomorrow. That'll be better."

Fine, I said, and went back to my table. I listened to a couple of more numbers and then left. Brady's Blues Lounge on Forty-seventh Street wasn't far away. I decided to go there and hear Valerie Wellington sing.

Brady's was at 525 Forty-seventh Street, a couple of blocks down from the old 708 Club of three decades ago. Of course, Forty-seventh Street is in the heart of "Bronzetown," the neighborhood that was once the center of black life in Chicago. The corner of Forty-seventh Street and King Drive was, during the forties, the crossroads of the city's black community. "If you stood on the corner for three hours," wrote Chicago insurance man Dempsey Travis, "you could see people you had not seen for years."

The front room of Brady's is a liquor store, but through the back door is a fashionable bar that features live blues two nights a week. While I waited for the music to begin, I talked for a while with Brady Harden, Jr. He and his father own the bar. Before coming home to Chicago to help run the family business, Harden had been a salesman for IBM in Atlanta. But after a few years, the corporate life began to wear on him and he gave up his briefcase and went home. Oddly enough, he said, racism is less of a problem in Atlanta than it is in Chicago.

"In Atlanta, I could live anywhere. I even lived in Stone Mountain. People told me, 'Don't live in Stone Mountain, man, that's where the Klan started. But I lived there and got along fine. Nobody bothered me. Here, in Chicago, it's not like that. There's still segregation, more than in Atlanta. Some parts of this town, a black man's just not welcome.

"We've had live music here for three years. I originally

thought of it as a vehicle for a lot of the local blues artists, particularly those right here in the neighborhood. What happened is that about three years ago Buddy Scott, who lives right down the street, and I talked quite a bit and came up with the idea one day of just throwing a little stage behind the bar. Then Buddy came in to play. It wasn't supposed to be a permanent thing, but it just snowballed. Buddy and Tyrone Davis's band played here for about eleven months. Now we have local blues twice a week.

"Of course, there's not as much blues on the South Side as there used to be. My father talks a lot about the old 708 Club, but that was a little before my time. That's where Muddy Waters, Little Walter, all the greats played. At one time, Forty-second Street was the bastion of the blues. And then Theresa's was across at Forty-eighth and Indiana. This neighborhood has a long, long history. We have a lot of people who came here from the South during the migration years, settled in this neighborhood and never moved.

"Now Blues, though, blues transcends all ethnicity. And it's been good for us for a lot of reasons. We made an album for Big Daddy Kinsey, and we're gonna start doing a lot of other things. I kinda feel like we're doing a service to the community by providing what they want. And I get a lot of enjoyment from it."

After an hour's wait, Valerie Wellington rushed in, streaking through the bar in jeans and a denim coat, carrying her costume trailing behind her. While she dressed, her band began to play. She is a former opera singer in her mid-twenties and a one-time Miss Black Chicago contestant who forsook Verdi and Wagner for Elmore James and Ma Rainey. She's made one record, but her greatest success has been a series of television commercials for the

Chicago Tribune where she shouts, "I don't want no puny paper."

When she began to sing, I knew she was one of the most powerful and expressive young blues singers I've heard in years, and it's no overstatement to compare her to Bessie Smith, Victoria Spivey, and Koko Taylor. Valerie is short, chocolate-brown, and her figure would have been more fashionable when models were curvy, not skinny and angular. At one point during the night, the power for her microphone went out. For some vocalists, that would have been the end of the show. Not for Valerie. She prowled up and down the bar, singing a cappella with enough force and emotion to make you weep. "You've got to give me some," she sang to every man at the bar, often holding on to his shoulder, "Please give me some." Her voice was full and rich, with overtones of the vaudeville blues of Bessie Smith. It lacked the harsh growl of Koko Taylor or Big Mama Willie Mae Thornton. It was authentic blues, but there was a hint of her formal musical training.

After the set she stopped by my table to talk.

"I started doing rhythm and blues stuff professionally when I was about twelve," she says as she sips her vodka and tonic and takes a deep drag off a menthol cigarette. "I was familiar with the music but you couldn't pay me to sing the blues back then. To me back then when I was twelve, it was like old people's music. I would never even touch that. But a lot of the blues artists worked the same clubs where I worked and I guess it rubbed off on me.

"Later, when I went to college, I didn't have anything to major in, so I figured I'd be a music major and play the piano, but my dad said I ought to be a voice major. At the school and all, it was just classical and jazz, basically, and I kinda liked opera and I got into that. I was in *L'Elisir d'Amore* by Donizetti, *Suor Angelica* by Puccini, and *La Clemenza di Tito* by Mozart. But while I was doing that, I'd go out to clubs and listen to the blues and it just kinda grew on me."

She takes another drag off her cigarette. "Later on, I had to make a decision—blues or opera. I prefer singing the blues, but every now and then I still run down to Orchestra Hall when everybody sings along with "The Messiah" and try out my stuff there. Opera is good music, and I appreciate it, but it's not for me to sing. In the long run I'd be making more singing opera, but, you know, in opera you don't really get to do major parts until you're in your late thirties or forties when your voice settles for that type of music. That's why the great ones are so far up in age. It's good music and I still love it and appreciate it, but I really didn't have the feeling for it."

As Valerie sips her vodka, she talks about her brief theatrical career—she played Ma Rainey in *The Little Dreamer: A Nite in the Life of Bessie Smith*. It's probably no coincidence that the first song on her only record album is "Down in the Dumps," the last song Bessie Smith ever recorded. "As far as the blues goes, I went from one extreme to the other, I started with the rural blues and worked my way up to B. B. King," she says. "But I was more influenced by the blues from the 1920s and the 1930s than what you'd hear now. Like Son House said, blues is really a music of lyrics. The music should follow the words. That's one reason I like the old vaudeville stuff that Bessie did, you know, the classic blues. They had a different sense of timing. But it was still the blues. But even then, you know, blues wasn't just for black people. Ma Rainey used to sing at white parties. Of course Bessie had a bigger white audience because Ma Rainey played mostly in tent shows in the South and in Chicago while Bessie was more New York. That was the days of the great minstrel shows with comedians, actors, dancers, everything.

"You know, I don't think I sound like a singer from Mississippi. I'm straight Midwest. I think my phrasing is a lot different, but still, even though it's very classical, it's gospel influenced. But I guess it might be pushing it to make such a big differentiation between voice and lyric. It's still the blues."

I stayed as long as she sang and went home in the early morning hours.

The next morning I thought about what Purvis Spann had said about the blues having no appeal to young blacks. Maybe that was true, but surely, judging from Valerie Wellington the night before, there were exceptions to Spann's rule. I'd heard of a man named Billy Branch who was working within the Chicago school system, teaching kids their blues heritage. I decided to give him a call. I did, and he invited me to his home on the corner of Ninety-sixth and Euclid, once again deep into the South Side.

Billy Branch is a handsome thirty-six-year-old black man with light skin and intense, pale-blue eyes. Branch is one of Chicago's premier blues harmonica players. He has his own band, The Sons of Blues, and he's played as a sideman on a lot of records.

"I started out working with kids as a blues artist in residence for the Illinois Art Council," Branch says in a husky, modulated voice. "I heard there were some blues artists in a residency program and I applied. At the time, I was working a day gig at Woolworth's, as a matter of fact. I got fired after we went on a tour to Berlin. And then this blues thing opened up.

"They gave me a pretty nice budget and I would instruct the kids in playing the harmonica. I had a partner with me, a guy named Shelly Fisher and he taught piano. He wasn't really a blues man but he was able to help teach the kids the basics. And so we would cultivate the kids with the history of the blues, then we would instruct them in piano, harmonica, or various percussion instruments. The kids would give concerts and sometimes we'd bring in guest artists like Sunnyland Slim or Jimmy Walker.

"I did that for about three years and during that time I received an offer from Urban Gateways, where I work now. It's more of a concert thing rather than giving classes. We don't really teach 'em field hollers, but we go through that a little. It's almost like a skit type of movement where I tell the kids to imagine if you are a slave, you didn't have any freedom, you had to work in the sun all day, get up before sunrise. We travel from school to school. And we invite 'em to come up onstage, make up their own blues songs—that sort of thing. We do a standard thing to teach them, we call it Homework Blues. It goes:

> *Didn't do my homework today, can't go out and play;*
> *Didn't do my homework today, can't go out and play.*
> *I feel so bad,*
> *Just like a ballgame on a rainy day.*

"And, you know, we do that call-and-response thing and then we do it with the harmonica and guitar and answer back and forth. You know," Billy says as he takes a swallow of coffee, "I'm still trying to figure out how I got so involved with the blues tradition. I was born in Chicago but I moved to L.A. when I was a kid. I picked up the harmonica when I was eleven or twelve years old. Then I came back to go to college. And when I did, I found this blues scene and I just—it was just something in me, man. It was like this was—me. And I was in love with it ever since. When I was on the West Coast, I never thought about being a musician. My goal was to be a lawyer. I came back here to Circle College and majored in political science.

"Lately, our band has been working on the South Side, probably more than most. We work the Raven Lounge on Eighty-eighth Street. Next weekend we do Rosa's on West Armitage—that's the club Homesick James's wife manages. We even worked Tate's—one of the big discos. At the Raven Lounge, we're the only blues band to work there steadily. And I had two spots on East Seventy-ninth Street. These weren't traditionally blues audiences. We develop them. They were kinda cold when we first came in. It might take two months to develop them. I do it partially to prove a point, because we've been playing in clubs that don't feature blues. I felt like if you brought it to them and had a good product, they'd have to appreciate it. And we proved that you could get a black crowd and a younger crowd to get into the blues. I run into people all the time who come up to me and say, 'I didn't like the blues until I heard you all.' And I tell them, 'You really liked it, you just didn't know you liked it.'

"The thing about the North Side is that it's—what can I say—it's like everybody's fighting for gigs. It's so much competition that they have the same people over and over—and basically, the club owners don't treat you with respect. Some club owners make the money—it's obvious they make plenty of money—and they just don't pay you enough. I mean, just say if you're charging three dollars on the door and you've got a turnover crowd of anywhere between two and three hundred people. Well, hey, that adds up. Well the most you can get would be four hundred dollars tops. And this is for a four- or five-man group. There was a time when they wanted you to work for the door and give you a percentage of the bar. Now that they've got the crowd so good, they don't even want to give you the door. I played the North Side for years and years and it's like now these guys have got their thing going and they don't need you. Especially when you're gonna stand up for what you believe in and let it be known that there are certain things you will accept and other things you won't.

"Basically," Branch said, "I don't have to change my music for a white audience, but occasionally with a black audience you might get more into rhythm and blues and oldies. If we got a nice group going, we might go into some Temptations and stuff. The white audience is somewhat getting into the same thing. It used to be that purist thing—if it's not blues we don't like it. I felt like they didn't understand that it's all blues, just different shades of blue. Naturally, those of us who are younger, our background is that we came up listening to Motown and James Brown. And all that is gonna be an influence.

"You know, there's more young black musicians interested in the blues now than when I first came on the scene. I've seen guys that, when I was kinda like doing my apprenticeship, just wanted to play funk. And I used to say, 'Play the blues. Play the blues,' because, you see, if you can play the blues, the funk is already there. Funk is not hard to play, it's just that James Brown feeling. But it comes out of the blues, it's just different timing and phrasing. Those same guys who wanted to play funk, they're all in blues bands now.

"It's basically true that for the last fifteen years the

blues was supported by white folks who wanted to hear it. And that's where you get these radio stations that won't play blues. Even so-called blues stations are not giving access to local talent. You know, you've got your fixtures— B. B. King, Little Milton, Albert King, Bobby Blue Bland, Z. Z. Hill, and for the most part that's it. It doesn't make sense to me. Because, especially in Chicago, you've got nine-tenths of the black population that came from the South and most of them from Mississippi.

"But there's a little progress being made. Robert Cray signed with Polydor. When has a bluesman signed with a major label since the 1950s? And then you've got Stevie Ray Vaughn, who to a lot of us isn't really the blues. But they're playing his records. I guess it's like a trickle-down theory—if somebody gets in there, maybe a few more will slip in. It seems to me you've got a tappable market. But the black stations will not play the blues. That's the major problem. You know Willie Dixon who used to work with Chess Records, who wrote most of the blues standards? I think he's one of the most outspoken philosophers of the music. He can really verbalize the essence of the blues. At one point he had a plan to go to the FCC and say that there was a conspiracy to keep the blues off the radio. I think the ramifications of that are kinda deep.

"Sometimes it feels like missionary work because you're up against such big odds—no airplay, no major media coverage. People at the black radio stations are the first to say, 'Oh, yeah, we love the blues.' But they won't play it because we're in this high-tech mass-media world where the blues doesn't fit in. Dealing with the children, it gives you a good feeling because it's like transmitting the culture. Carrying a torch might be an exaggeration. It's like telling a story—because the blues is just a story put to music. And the story involves history and hard times. I feel that the essence of black culture is locked up inside the blues." He pauses a moment and then smiles. "But it doesn't just involve black culture," he adds. "Look at Howard Hughes. A billionaire who died of starvation while he was wearing Kleenex boxes on his feet. That's the blues, man."

Branch is indeed a missionary, I thought, as I headed back downtown. He's working against incredible odds to recreate a past that's faded away. And, I realized, I'd been doing the same thing. It was natural to want to find the small, dark clubs that had nurtured blues heroes like the fabled Muddy Waters and Howlin' Wolf, but the scene has changed.

Except for trying to talk to Magic Slim one more time, I decided not to indulge in any more nostalgia. The blues in Chicago is on the North Side now. In years to come there may be as much nostalgia for Biddy Mulligan's, Wise Fool's, Kingston Mines, and B.L.U.E.S as there is now for Theresa's, the 708 Club, and Pepper's Lounge.

One of the best-known North Side Clubs, although certainly not the oldest, is B.L.U.E.S. So I made arrangements to have dinner with Bill Gilmore, the owner. We ate at Fricano's, a tasty Italian restaurant across Halsted Street from his place. Between bites of veal, he talked about his club and the blues in Chicago.

"You've got to understand something about the blues in this town," Gilmore said, "although I'm sure other people have told you this or you've already figured it out. Middle-class blacks do not listen to the blues. They listen to jazz. Middle-class blacks would be as likely to go to a blues bar as someone with pretense to class in the South would be to go to a roadhouse to hear country-and-western music. It's changing a little because the middle-class white community says blues is OK, and so blacks may start listening now.

"The South Side blues clubs that have survived do it mainly with white audiences. They have very minimal expenses. The only club that's really drawn consistently well on the South Side in the last ten years is the Checkerboard. And on the weekend it'll be seventy-five percent nonblack—white and Oriental.

"I've been running bars for ten years. I've only had three clubs and they've all been blues bars. The first was called Elsewhere on Lincoln Avenue. Then we had another Elsewhere on Clark. Actually, the first place, we didn't intend it to be a music bar. We just started out with a kind of neighborhood hangout that some friends of mine and I ran. And it sort of turned into a blues bar by osmosis. I had a friend who worked at Hull House and he was a piano player. He'd hung around with some of the older piano players—Sunnyland Slim, John Davis, Jimmy Walker—and he said to me, 'Well, I see you've got a piano in your window.' And we did. It was left over from the previous owner. And he asked if we'd mind if he came in on Saturday nights and play for tips.

"So we started with him. Then he told Jimmy Walker about the place and he came in on Fridays. Walker told Homesick James who played on Thursday night and he told Eddie Taylor and before you knew it, we had blues seven nights a week. It was totally unplanned. No cover, no minimum, incredibly cheap drinks. I mean like forty-cent beers. I mean cheap.

"I'd always listened to the blues. I listened a lot in the sixties, some in the seventies, but I really hadn't kept up. I'd gone to places like Pepper's, the old Big John's, and

Theresa's on the South Side. And, of course, the Checkerboard. That bar got a lot of help because it was owned by Buddy Guy, the blues guitar player. And, of course, some of the touring British rock stars knew Buddy and would go to the Checkerboard when they came to Chicago, and that helped. But I preferred Theresa's. I think I listened to blues in the sixties because if you had pretenses of being hip during those times, that's what you listened to. And I liked the bars, liked the atmosphere. I spent a lot of time in bars before I owned them. And then, for me, the blues was sort of exotic. I came from a very quiet background," Gilmore said.

"Anyway, Elsewhere was in a white working-class neighborhood about a mile from here. And we weren't terribly popular with people who lived there and people who ran other businesses. That was ten years ago. There's been a lot of development in this part of town since. Ten years ago, where we sit right now was working class. Now it's upper middle class.

"The main problem we had at Elsewhere was our landlord. He hated blacks and he hated Jews. And most of our musicians and customers were one or the other. So we went over to Clark Street. It was a much bigger space and we came up with the bright idea that since we were doing well with a small bar, we'd do much better with a bigger one. Wrong. It only lasted a year and a half and we lost a fair amount of money. The place was just too big. It was an old disco and it just never worked for the blues.

"In seventy-eight I got some new partners and they wanted to do a Rush Street thing, you know, tourists and all that, with the blues. I tried to tell them I don't think you want to do this. They said they knew how to run bars and I'm looking like a Grade-A jerk with my track record, so I said OK. I left.

"I stayed out of business until April of seventy-nine. I was putting out feelers and a friend came by and said, 'You've got to see this place over on Halsted Street. It looks just like the first Elsewhere.' Now, at this point, the first Elsewhere had become a legend. It was like seeing Muddy's band in 1953. So I went over to Halsted and walked in and, sure enough, it looked about like my first bar. Real close.

"It was a different design then. It didn't have the stage and it was a sort of college-hangout bar. Of course, we've expanded it a bit. We started booking blues there in late April. On the North Side our mainstream audience—I hate to use the word *yuppie* because a lot of our people are older—is white working professionals. It's really hard to say how much of our business is tourism, but we do have an international reputation. We get written up in French tourist books, English tourist books. That sort of developed in the last three or four years. If you have something in town like the Consumer Electronic Show, that brings in a hundred thousand people. And we get, oh, one-tenth of one percent. That's a lot of people for us, but it's nothing in terms of the show," Gilmore said.

"The crowds at B.L.U.E.S. are different from night to night. Sunday night, I guess it's more of a local crowd. Sunnyland Slim had that gig for five years and it's still our more traditional night. Weekends, we get a lot of people from the suburbs and from the neighborhood. Any heavy tourist business is during the summer.

"I think blues people look to us to see what we do. For example, somebody like Otis Clay didn't play the North

Side until I started booking him. He's got a little different style, more the style of the soul singer out in front of the band. And the North Side has always been guitar-oriented. For example, you never see Bobby Blue Bland on the North Side. With women it's a different thing. Big Time Sarah, Valerie, Koko, Gloria Hardiman, that's more accepted. Li'l Ed, I was booking him at our club four years before he made a record. Then of course Magic Slim, Jimmy Johnson, Son Seals—I book them. James Cotton comes through three or four times a year. There's a good talent pool here. Even in New York, if you want to hear blues, the Chicago guys are the headliners.

"The difference between a North Side club and one on the South Side, other than location, of course, is that our customers are very time-conscious. If you say the music's gonna start at eight-thirty or nine o'clock, you better be pretty close. People get irate if they've been here for an hour and haven't heard any music. I've been to places on the South Side where the music was supposed to start at nine. I get there at ten and the band hasn't even set up. And it might be another hour, hour and a half before they start playing. You might be hearing music by eleven-thirty. Of course, a lot of the time the South Side or West Side clubs are neighborhood bars. So if the band's a little late, the people from the neighborhood just play the jukebox. And the musicians live in the neighborhood, too. People leave the bar, go over and find 'em and bring 'em back. There's just a different sense of time on the South Side.

"Our club seats a hundred-ten. It's full every night. But if you gave me a big club, say four hundred-fifty seats, I only think I could fill it once a month. You could book Robert Cray, B. B. King when you could get him, Albert

King. They're all people who could fill the place. But if you asked me to name you twelve, I think I'd start stumbling. It's just not a mass-market music. I'd be very leery of booking blues in a club that seats more than two hundred.

"But it's more than the same grind every night. I mean, we do things like, well, for example, every July I do a blues festival and we do thirty-one different bands in thirty-one days. And we're just starting our own record label, too. So far we've recorded Otis Clay, Big Time Sarah, Johnny Dollar. We'll be doing more," Gilmore said.

"I guess we pay the musicians better than any other place in town on slow nights. And we pay less than some other clubs on good nights. Because we're small and durable, we wind up somewhere in the middle. I steer clear of giving a percentage of the gate. I used to do that, but I remember one guy who wanted a percentage of the door and every night he kept saying, 'I'm getting beat, I'm getting beat.' So one night I came in for the eleven o'clock show and worked the door the rest of the night. At the end of the night, I gave the guy the money from the door. It was easily two hundred dollars more than he'd make at any other place. But he starts yelling that I'm stealing his money, that the white man is always against the black man. I told him to get out. In the first place, that's not true. And in the second place, I don't have to put up with it."

Bill patted his lips with his napkin and took a last sip of coffee. "I think you have to remember why we're written up in all these tour guides. People like us. The thing about B.L.U.E.S. is that I book at a very high level. We're open three hundred-sixty-five days a year. You're not going to see something really bad. I think if you ask the experts, they'll say if you've only got one night in Chicago to hear the blues, go to B.L.U.E.S. And I think that's something to be proud of."

After dinner, we walked across the street to B.L.U.E.S. Son Seals was playing that night. I'd heard his records and he seemed to have a dark, threatening, mysterious presence. If Hawk, the character from Robert Parker's Spencer novels, was to become a bluesman, he would be like Son Seals.

The place was packed. Seals, who is a latter-day refugee from Mississippi, took command of the stage. His deep growls and sly laughs punctuated the lyrics and his piercing guitar playing. The music had the hard edge of the Chicago ghetto, a sharp, harsh sound that occasionally bordered on jazz when a clarinet player soloed. Although there was really no similarity, you could hear the faint undertones of old New Orleans jazz after musicians like Louis Armstrong, Lil Hardin, and King Oliver made their pilgrimage to Chicago.

Son Seals was a dark, mysterious presence as he stood wearing black, hunched over his guitar. He played song after song without smiling, although there was some humor in his music. I stuck around until he finished. Later, we had coffee at a diner downtown near the Jazz Record Mart. His dark, mysterious presence is mostly an act. His normal expression is still a scowl, but he talks and acts with the demeanor of a Southern gentleman.

"My dad, he used to play for the old *Rabbit Foot Minstrels*. That show went back, oh, maybe into the late twenties and all through the thirties. I think he was with them going into the late thirties because I was born in forty-two and by then he had pulled away from that and opened our own place in my hometown of Oceola, Arkansas.

"You have to be kinda up there in years to remember the minstrel show. In fact, you know I did get a chance to see it a few times because they had this thing where they would do a season—they would tour the South and all. They worked about four or five months out of the year. That had to be in the early fifties, somewhere around that time. I was big enough to remember it well. There was another one, Silas Green from New Orleans. It consisted of dancing girls, comedians, exotic dancers, all that kind of stuff. They had a big band, maybe thirteen to sixteen pieces. It was good too. Really an eye opener for me.

"Oceola, it sits right on the Mississippi about forty-five miles north of Memphis. I started playing real young. Being right in the middle of music, you might say I was raised up around it because my dad was running this little juke joint called the Dipsey Doodle. Especially on weekends, there was always some kind of entertainment. I got exposed to a lot of the guys when they were just gettin' started. Guys like like B. B. King, Robert Nighthawks, Joe Hill Louis, Bobby Blue Bland. All these guys who started off in the Memphis area played my hometown. And by us living in the back of the place, I had a chance to be right there when it was going on. If it hadn't been for that, being exposed to it, who knows? I might have been a doctor now.

"But as a kid growing up, all that music rubbed off on me and I wanted to play, too. And my dad—he played guitar, piano, a little drums, trombones, and stuff—was a lot of help to me. When I first started trying to fool around on the guitar, he showed me my first few licks. So that's as far back as I can remember.

"Back then places didn't have to close up at any certain time like they do now and the music would go all night. They played till they'd fall out and then just quit. There was no such thing as getting up onstage to do a forty-five-minute or an hour set. They just played. And I lost a lot of sleep listening. I used to sneak around and fool with some of the guys' stuff. One man by the name of Odell Mitchell, he was a drummer—and I started out playing drums. He used to leave his drum set at the club and I used to mess around with it whenever he wasn't there. And at that time, WBIA, the black radio station in Memphis, played nothing but blues around the clock. Plus the fact that there was a jukebox in the place and every time I got a hold a two or three nickels, I'd play the blues. That was what I had to practice with. Every chance I got I'd be up there with the radio on, fooling around with the drums. I picked it up pretty easy. I guess it was in me to play. Once the guys found out I could play a little, they'd sometimes let me sit in. I'm so short I'm behind the drums and you can hardly see me. Joe Hill Louis, as a matter of fact, was one who I played with. He was one of the men from Memphis who did the one-man band. He had his stuff all rigged with guitar and snare drum—he could play the high hat and the snare drum at the same time. And I asked my dad if I could sit in and play something, and he said, 'Yeah, go on back there.' Well, Joe Hill Louis, he liked it so well to where every Monday night he'd come in and use me on the drums instead of playing it himself. I guess that's what triggered it off. But I was young, man. Some of the other guys would come in and ask my dad if they could take me out and play certain places with 'em. And I'd go out and play these parties. Back then there wasn't too much of a teenage or young white audience like there is now. What was popular was Nat King Cole's kind of jump blues. There wasn't any rock and roll back then. Even though these white kids liked to dance, they wasn't into the kind of stuff we was doing for black people. They were into, oh, a Fats Domino tune or anything close to bop. I guess I never would have learned 'Stardust,' 'Deep Purple,' or 'Smoke Gets In Your Eyes'—all that kind of stuff—had it not been for playing those parties.

"One old guy, I remember, he must have been well into his sixties, his name was Johnny Moore. You talk about a piano player! And so by playing around him I kinda learned to go across the board. I could bat on both sides of the plate. Somebody come along and need a man to play country and western, whatever, I could do it. Because I played with a country-western band there for a while. I was the only black guy that was doing it. They said they needed a drummer and I said, 'I'm your man.' And I'm glad I did. Not only did it show me what I really liked to play, but it gave me a chance to get some experience in all fields of music," Seals said.

"The blues, though, that's what I liked best. That came from being more exposed to blues and playing it more than anything else, plus being around men like Albert King, who was living in my hometown at that time. Then there were all the musicians coming over from Memphis. My dad played blues but it wasn't like what we do now—he played some of that old stuff, New Orleans deep-South blues—like you'd hear behind Bessie Smith. I enjoyed it, but I knew I couldn't play it.

"Albert King moved to St. Louis in the late fifties and he started to tour. Every once in a while he'd come back home. One night he came down there and he needed a drummer. So I played with him and he asked me to tour with him. And I said, 'Well, my dad, man, I don't know.' But I talked to my daddy and because he knew Albert and had known him so long, he said yes. Anybody else, I don't think he would have gone along with it. I guess I was nineteen or twenty, it ain't like I was a baby. But still, I wasn't legally of age. But then my dad took sick on me and I went back home to take care of him and stayed there until he died.

"See, prior to going out on the road with Albert, I already had my little group together. We had been working all around the area, up in Missouri, Tennessee, Little Rock, Hot Springs. We'd work anywhere within two hundred miles around. I kinda did both, drums and guitar. In fact, by the time Albert came along and picked me up, I was already playing guitar. And he liked it. He always said when I find somebody good on them drums boy, I'm gonna put you on that guitar where you belong. But my daddy had a stroke and so I stayed around there. He was still running the place and I knew he needed my help. After he passed in seventy-one, I moved here to Chicago.

"I came here sometimes with Albert, and I came here to visit. My sister's here and all—and her husband Joe, he was a blues fanatic. He'd take me everywhere he could think of to get me to meet people. He's responsible for me meeting Hound Dog Taylor in the sixties. That was one reason why I chose Chicago, because I figured if I'm gonna make a move to any of these cities and be in music, Chicago was the place. It was a big city but it was just like being at home musically. After a while, I found out that all the musicians I ran into were from down South—you know, Howlin' Wolf, Muddy Waters. Chicago is where it was happening. I played with Wolf and Muddy and Jimmy Reed at the old Pepper's Lounge on East Forty-third Street. Getting tied up with Hound Dog was responsible for a lot of that. Playing behind him gave people a chance to see me and know my work. I have to give Hound Dog a lot of credit. When I first met him, back in the 1960s, I sat in with him for a while. He knew my brother-in-law real well—they'd drink together and shoot the bull, and Hound Dog didn't forget me, either. I moved here in seventy-one and went into the Expressway Lounge on Fifty-fifth Street where he was playing. He looked up and said, 'There's Son Seals.' I played with him some that night and gave him my phone number.

"A week or two later, him and his guitar player fell out. They was always doing that and so he got me to play with him. I played with him four or five weeks until Bruce Iglauer came along and told Hound Dog he'd booked him on the road for a while. Hound Dog come in and told me that if I could get a few guys together, we could hold down the gig. So three of us started at the Expressway Lounge and we played three or four months there before a friend of Bruce's, Wesley Race, was in there one night listening to us play. He got excited and called Bruce and let him listen to us over the phone. And the next Saturday night Bruce Iglauer of Alligator Records showed up.

"He told me, 'If you will get your guys together and work up some tunes of your own, and then call me and let me check it out, I want to make a record.' I said OK. I thought maybe he was jivin'—I heard all this before. But one day a couple of weeks later, sure enough, Bruce called and we set a rehearsal. He came over and liked what he heard. And I been recording and touring ever since," Seals said.

"The blues in Chicago may have changed over the years because you got more young guys playing. A lot of young players are coming on and they got a lot more fire and energy than the laid-back guys. People come up and say, 'It's almost like rock and roll'—and I say, 'Where you think rock and roll came from?' It's all because of the energy level. Some people think the blues has got to be all laid back and crying in your beer. If you had come up like I did and saw what was going on, you'd know the people didn't come out and moan and groan. They had problems, yeah, but on Saturday nights until half of Sunday, they'd go out and have a good time. You couldn't see them for the dust. They'd be enjoying themselves and forgetting their anxieties and tensions. People who don't know that expect the blues to always be laid back.

"Lot of those old South Side places just closed up. And if they didn't close down, they went disco. It got to be so that everybody thought, hell, I can get a guy to come in and spin some records and charge four or five dollars at the door. And that did work for a while. You go to these places and they'd be really going over big. And the music never did work its way back. Nowadays, when you get past Forty-third street, it's all over. Now it's North Side clubs.

"It used to be that playing on the North Side was a rarity. It didn't happen. Only every once in a while. We either played on the South Side or we'd go out of town. I hated to see what happened to the South Side happen, but the North Side is fine. Lot of people back years ago had already heard of the Checkerboard and they'd say, 'Is it cool to go there or to Theresa's?' Now when they ask me that, I have to say to go see who's playing at Kingston Mines, B.L.U.E.S., Biddy Mulligan's, Wise Fool's."

The next evening, I drive back over to the Checkerboard, hoping that maybe I can get Magic Slim to talk. It costs four dollars to get in and there's no band playing. What the hell? I pay it anyway and go inside. Two old men are sitting near the entrance, drinking beer and playing whist. Pop music blares from the jukebox. At the bar, Magic Slim sits alone, drinking Wild Turkey, beer as a chaser.

I sat down on a bar stool next to him. Except for us, the old men playing cards, and a couple of other guys hanging around the men's-room door, the place was deserted. Where was the crowd of the weekend? What happened?

"Well," says Slim, knocking back his bourbon and ordering another, "nah—the place haven't changed. It haven't changed. Nah. It's about the same system. I don't know if they'll be much of a crowd. Weekdays are kinda slow. Then sometimes, they're not. You never can tell. See, we don't play until they's a crowd. Last night, we sat here until about eleven o'clock. And then all at once come a busload. A goddamn busload of tourists. This place was packed. We get lots of tourists in here. Last week it was packed with people from Japan."

He lapsed into silence and we both sat there, staring straight ahead, not looking at each other.

"Has the blues changed much in the last few years?" I finally ask.

He thinks about it for a while. During the silence, I'm afraid he's forgotten my question.

"Well," he finally answered, "the notes be the same. Things are changin' but the blues, the blues ain't changin'. See, I'm trying to do what I do and do what I know but I'm trying to do it better. You see, I play some of my notes more plainer and some of 'em faster and some of 'em slower. But you got to practice to play them clearer. If you play them all together, it'll be all fuzzy. Peoples will hear 'em, but they won't be able to figure out the differences."

More silence. I sip my drink, Slim sips his.

"Not as many places to play blues on the South Side as there used to be," I say.

"Well, there's a lot of places you can buy booze, but ain't too many still handling blues. But you know, it still feel good though. There's just as much interest in blues now as there ever was. I'm puttin' a little more in it now. I like to play the blues anyway. I'm playin' them harder. You know, the little bit I know. I been trying to play them harder. But you know, black folks still like the blues. Yeah, they like it. Lots of black folks ain't got no money. They can't afford to come out every night because they got to work. But mostly on weekends, they go as many places as they can."

He lapses into silence again and we both stare at the front door, waiting for the tour bus. I waited for an hour and a half. No bus. I get up to leave.

"See you around," says Slim.

I drove back to the North Side and stopped in at the Wise Fool's Pub, a couple of blocks away from B.L.U.E.S. on North Lincoln. Li'l Ed and the Blues Imperials are playing there. If Slim represents the old-time Chicago bluesman, Li'l Ed is the new breed. Ed Williams is only thirty-two and is a native of Chicago. He never migrated anywhere. His blues route was from a six-dollar-a-night gig at Big Duke's on the West Side to the more lucrative North Side clubs.

Ed's onstage when I walk in. The band's music emphasizes Li'l Ed's slide guitar and a heavy boogie beat. Little Ed walks into the audience on his knees, then does back-flips. He never misses a note. He is wearing a furry fez that was made from an ice bucket by his aunt, who is a hotel maid. He's slim and stands just over five feet tall. The music sounds like Chicago blues, but it's innovative, and sometimes Ed's slide guitar has overtones of a pedal steel guitar, giving the music rockabilly or country overtones.

After he finishes, Ed and I go into the next room and talk during intermission.

"I been playing ever since I was about fourteen year old," he tells me breathlessly. "That's when I first started out. My uncle was teaching me. He was J. D. Hutto. You know about him?"

Sure, I do. He moved to Chicago from South Carolina, won the Downbeat Critic's Award in 1969, wrote the 'Chicago Boogie' and the 'Diabetic Blues,' among others. Hell of a teacher to have.

"I even listen some to country music," Ed says. "I try to get some of that Hawaiian stuff in what I play. During the daytime, I work as a buffer at the Red Carpet Car Wash on West Washington Street. Car-wash work and working at night playing is kinda rough on me because, especially in the blues racket, a musician's life just isn't that stable. I'm waiting for the music to pick up.

"Man, this album is the best thing that ever happened to me. We went in there to do one song—we had been playing at B.L.U.E.S. and Bruce asked us to go to the studio so we could have one number on this album of young blues singers—and we just started jamming and we did about fifteen or sixteen songs. We went on and cut about thirty songs in two hours. Bruce gave us a contract with Alligator. Right there.

"After listening to my uncle sing all these blues, I really like what he did. I don't have any temptation to play anything but the blues. I may play a little in the country style sometimes, I may do a little Bobby Blue Bland every once in a while. But I don't want to imitate B. B. King. I want to be Li'l Ed. One B. B. King is enough."

He excused himself and went back for another set.

In Chicago, the blues is still an exciting, driving force. Maybe it's not the same, but what is? Hoping the music wouldn't change is like playing old swing records all the time and refusing to listen to anything else. In jazz they used to call people like that moldy figs.

In Chicago, at least, the figs aren't moldy. And the blues is not in a museum. It's alive and vibrant. Maybe it's not everybody's music, but when Muddy Waters was at the height of his popularity, most people listened to Frank Sinatra instead. Any talk of the death of the blues is premature. Take away the respirator, Doc. I think the patient's gonna live.

Dockery Farms, where the blues was born

Lynn White

Bo Diddley

Son Thomas

Rufus Thomas

Koko Taylor

James Cotton

Valerie Wellington Blues Band

Son Seals

JACINTA MERRILL

Lil' Ed Williams
and the Blues Imperials

Bruce Iglauer

JACINTA MERRILL

Dirty Dozen Brass Band

Rockin' Dopsie

C. J. Chenier

Mark Savoy

Eddie "Cleanhead" Vinson

The Johnny Otis Show

Jimmy and Jeannie Cheatham

Margie Evans

JACINTA MERRILL

Jimmy McCracklin

JACINTA MERRILL

4

THE JUDGE AND I were speeding though Gulfport and Pass Christian and Biloxi with a bottle of Dixie Beer in each hand and a stripper between us. The Judge was driving his old white Thunderbird faster than either God or Mississippi law ever intended, because we were in a hurry to get to New Orleans.

It was a celebration for all three of us. For the Judge it was a chance to get away from the somber confines of small-town judicial tasks; for me it was a weekend away from three deadlines a day and a screaming city editor; for the Stripper it was a toast to her last weekend with small breasts—Monday she would be surgically augmented in an effort to revive what she was afraid was a faltering career.

We found the Stripper along the way in a small Mississippi town and, like us, she was dreaming of New Orleans. It was where she wanted to work, and with her new implants she thought she might one day be as famous as Tempest Storm or Blaze Starr.

"Hey, Judge, pop us another beer. Nothing like this has ever happened before. They don't have strippers waiting for surgery in Opp or Jasper and damn few in Birmingham. And we've got one in the T-Bird with us going to New Orleans."

We ate too much that weekend, drank too much, had to spend a couple of wobbly hours outrunning some city detectives for reasons best forgotten, and the Stripper paid for the whole thing. We listened to jazz and rhythm and blues and we cheered when Frog Man Henry sang like a girl and then croaked like a frog. Three days later, satiated with sin and cursed with headaches and cotton mouth, we let the Stripper out at a Mississippi hospital and turned the T-Bird toward Alabama.

I remembered that weekend from years ago as I headed south through those same coastal towns on a mission to find what's left of the blues in New Orleans. I was older and balder than I had been on that lost weekend, but I was not sure I was any wiser. New Orleans still had the lure of delicious sin and I began to look forward to Oysters Rockefeller, café au lait, Shrimp Arnaud, and maybe an encounter with that same stripper—more curvaceous now but, in my mind, still in her twenties.

Delicious sin has always been one of New Orleans's major cash crops. At the turn of the century, it was Storyville, the legalized red-light district that gave the city its reputation. It was named after Alderman Sidney Story who authored legislation confining prostitution to one district and making it legal. Block after block of the city, in an area adjoining the French Quarter, was set aside for whorehouses.

"Those places were really something to see," pianist Clarence Williams told Nat Shapiro and Nat Hentoff in their oral history of jazz, *Hear Me Talkin' to Ya*.

They had the most beautiful parlors, with cut glass and draperies, and rugs, and expensive furniture. They were just like millionaires' houses.

And the girls would come down dressed in the finest of evening gowns, just like they were going to the opera. They were just beautiful. Their hair-dos were just so, and I'm telling you that Ziegfeld didn't have any more beautiful women than these. Some of them looked Spanish and some were Creoles, some brownskin, some chocolate brown. But they all had to have that figure.

The most famous of the opulent bordellos was Lulu White's Mahogany Hall. A promotional booklet put out by Madam White called it, "The handsomest house of its kind. It's the only one where you can get three shots for your money—the shot upstairs, the shot downstairs, and the shot in the room."

In addition to the sensual delights at houses like The Arlington, Mahogany Hall, Diane and Norma's French House, and Countess Willie V. Piazza's, there was the music. In the whorehouses themselves, it was mostly piano music, played by "professors" like Tony Jackson and Jelly Roll Morton. But in nearby saloons like Pete Lala's place, you could hear early jazz.

"I would delight delivering an order of stone coal to the prostitute who used to hustle in her crib next to Pete Lala's cabaret," Louis Armstrong said in an interview in *True* magazine;

Just so's I could hear King Oliver play. I was too young to go in Pete Lala's at that time. And I'd just stand there in that lady's crib listening to King Oliver. All of a sudden it would dawn on that lady that I was still in her crib very silent while she hustle those tricks and she'd say—'What's the matter with you, boy. Why are you standing so quiet. This is no place to dream. I've got my work to do.'

Storyville closed in 1917, but its reputation lingered —both as an urban garden of delights and as an early home of jazz. Over the years as prostitution spread out all over town, the music of the city changed from jazz to rhythm and blues.

"In the decade following World War II, many musics colored New Orleans," according to Jason Berry's *Up from the Cradle of Jazz*, a history of New Orleans music:

The French Quarter was the big strip, and the music varied from traditional jazz to respectable white Dixieland and the sugary accents of swing. The Quarter appealed to more than musical interests, however. New Orleans was a wide-open town where a savvy tourist with a roll of bills could find a gambling joint or a slot machine if he knew how to be subtle, and willing ladies if he wasn't so subtle.

But beyond Bourbon Street, there was once again new music being created. In East New Orleans at Natal's, you could hear the beginning of rhythm and blues in the music of Edgar Blanchard and the Gondoliers. On the Gentilly Highway, Shirley and Lee and Frankie Ford played at the Safari Room. These were the days of segregation, however, and while blacks could perform at these places, they couldn't be served. So a new type of club was born and with it, a freer music.

According to *Up from the Cradle of Jazz*:

To these clubs gravitated a society unto itself. An oasis of night people—jazz players, singers, shake-dancers, an occasional movie star, drag queens, snake charmers, bohemians from the Quarter and countless other character types who lived in a different world. Upper and middle class blacks came for quality music and dance. Music was the central force, the raison d'être, of the Dew Drop Inn, Club Tiajuana and other places of the early rhythm-and-blues years. The clubs also served elemental human needs.

In turn, the great days of rhythm and blues faded as surely as Storyville did. Only it wasn't the law that brought them down. It was rock and roll, the new music that ate everything it came in contact with and homogenized it for the taste of white teenagers.

New Orleans is famous for jazz, of course, but mixed with that jazz is the soul of the blues that lived on at places like the Dew Drop. If jazz was still in New Orleans, I figured as I shook the memories of the Judge and the Stripper from my mind, the blues would have to be there, too.

There are people who would doubt that Mississippi is the home of the blues. They think New Orleans is where it all started, despite the conclusions of historical research. They cite a 1946 song by Louis Armstrong, "Where the Blues Was Born in New Orleans." The song is only blue in its title, although it's a Tin Pan Alley composition that strikes not one blue note, but this is the gospel for some people, the musical equivalent of Genesis. These people say they love the blues. For them, the blues grew out of the early jazz traditions and those, of course, came from New Orleans. Maybe they've got a point about the origins of the blues—or at least a point about the early documentation of the music. In his book, *Mr. Jelly Roll*, Alan Lomax quotes Jelly Roll Morton, the New Orleans pianist, as remembering the blues when he talked about his days as a musician in the whorehouses of Storyville:

> And then there was the Game Kid just swilling all the lush in the world. He was a howler, I'm telling you, the best there was in the section when it came to playing the blues.

And Morton also remembered Mamie Desdoumes:

> Two middle fingers of her right hand had been cut off, so she played the blues with only three fingers on her right hand . . . it was Mamie first really sold me on the blues.

So before 1917, blues was being played in the fabled whorehouses of New Orleans. That was a long time before Charley Patton ever recorded the Mississippi blues. Maybe it was in the brothels that blues became associated with dirty songs. Even today the music has a supercharged sexual content. As Pigiron, an Atlanta blues disc jockey, once told me, "I've heard of double entendre, all right—but these blues, they don't have but one entendre."

It's only logical that the blues would make their way down the Mississippi from the Delta, as well as north by rail to Chicago. South was how the Mississippi flowed. But the blues was not the dominant sound in New Orleans. As Al Rose says in his book, *Storyville, New Orleans*:

> The type of vocal blues made famous by Ma Rainey, Bessie Smith, and countless others was not

indigenous to New Orleans and was not prominent in Storyville's musical picture, but at least one such singer, Ann Cook, did perform in the District, as did the celebrated song-and-dance man Willie Jackson, who included such blues songs as "Bad, Bad Mama," "She Keeps It Up All the Time," and "Willie Jackson's Blues" in his regular cabaret routine.

The New Orleans bluesmen played piano, not guitar, although there's some small evidence of string bands in Storyville. It was the "professor" at his piano in the fabled brothels who became the representative performer.

What Storyville was able to accomplish, however, was a breakdown of the caste systems between Creoles and blacks. As Alan Lomax wrote in his biography of Jelly Roll Morton:

By and large these black Americans [among the musicians] were common laborers or service workers. They were not trained musicians, but won their Storyville jobs by sheer talent. Creoles who wanted to work in Storyville had to play in bands with them. So, for the first time since Reconstruction, Creoles were forced to accept blacks as equals and this was bitter medicine. . . . There was fear and hate on both sides, but jazz demanded cooperation.

And it was this cooperation that made the blues a part of jazz.

Back then, New Orleans was ashamed of its musical heritage. In the 1938 WPA Guide to New Orleans, jazz takes up only four of sixteen pages devoted to music. The rest of the chapter is devoted to classical music, particularly opera. Says the directory:

> New Orleans has often been said to be the birth-place of jazz, the outgrowth of cacophony turned out by "spasm" bands which made their appearance in the last decade of the nineteenth century. Playing in front of saloons, theaters, and brothels of the city, these bands regaled the public with their informal "ear" music. However abhorrent the clamor produced by this assortment of instruments might have seemed to music-loving Orleanians, the band attained sufficient popularity by 1911 to warrant an engagement in New York.

The shame only passed when the city became tourist-conscious. Now you can hear re-creations of the jazz played in the brothels and bars of Storyville in French Quarter storefronts like Preservation Hall. But that's museum music. The performers are alive, but they are not much more imaginative then automatons at Disney World.

"There's not much blues in New Orleans," Ben Sandmill, a writer for *Downbeat*, told me, "but it's a real bluesy city."

He's right, but for a strange reason: Blues is indigenous to American culture; New Orleans is an amalgam of French and Caribbean roots, no matter what the atlas shows. The blues came from the fields of cotton plantations; it never gained any respectability—it was a subculture of its own. In New Orleans, Creole society, which was often made up of families that were part black, part

French, was as refined as its white counterpart. Before the Civil War, there were free blacks and Creoles of color in New Orleans who were in most of the professions and businesses. Among those Creoles, there was a strong musical tradition. According to Al Rose, the French Opera was attended mostly by Creoles when they played the city. So the music heard in Creole households, where a piano was not uncommon, was more likely to be French quadrilles than the "Tiger Rag," the jazz standard based on one of those classical tunes. Add to that the influences of Haitian refugees who brought not only their voodoo religion but Caribbean rhythms as well and you see why the blues was only a small part of the African musical heritage in New Orleans.

"There was a caste system in New Orleans," Danny Barker, a veteran jazzman, told Nat Hentoff:

> Each of those castes had its own trumpet player, and Chris Kelly played for those blues, cotton-picking Negroes, what they called in the old days "yard and field Negroes." They were real primitive people who worked in the fields, worked hard. He was a master and played more blues than anyone you ever knew. New Orleans, through the years, had some thirty-odd halls. Each of these halls had a different class distinction based on color, family standing, money and religion. The most exclusive was the Jean Ami, where very few jazz men ever entered—down to the Animal Hall, where even a washboard band was welcome if they could play the blues. So Chris Kelly, who was dark of color, low on finance, Baptist from birth and

educated in the canebrakes, never gave a thought to ever blowing his blues in the Jean Ami Hall. He talked a real broken patois, African almost. The Creoles couldn't understand him. They didn't like him and they didn't want to see him in the street, because he played for what was supposed to be the bad element.

New Orleans blues was not pure. It became a part of jazz, although in the 1920s, the words *blues* and *jazz* were interchangeable in the minds of many people. Blues, ragtime, formal French music, and marching bands combined to make up jazz. Once the mixture was blended, it was hard to separate the elements again.

Take Professor Longhair, the rockin' piano player who was the spiritual if not the linear successor to the whorehouse "professors" of Storyville. He was often classified as a blues musician, but there is a second-line beat in his playing that can be distinguished from rhythm-and-blues music heard anywhere else in the country. New Orleans music is like Creole cooking—part black, part European, part West Indian. It is the mixture that gives it a special quality.

All this talk of early jazz is not meant to slight the rhythm and blues that came from this "Caribbean" city. Fats Domino lived here and so did Huey Piano Smith, Ernie K-Doe, Shirley and Lee, Smiley Lewis, Sugar Boy and the Sugar Lumps, Irma Thomas, Papa Jellie Bellie and his Original Jolly Bunch, and a rhythm-and-blues female impersonator named Bobby Marchan. New Orleans is the home of Dr. John the Night Tripper, Allen Toussaint, the Neville Brothers, and Mardi Gras Indian bands like the Wild Magnolias and the Wild Tchoupitoulas. The city is awash with music, but if it's blues, it's blues transformed.

Actually, music is part of New Orleans's main industry: the continuous, nonstop party. Ever since the United Fruit Company rerouted the banana boats to Mobile and the oil industry hit the skids, party time is about all the city has left. And they do it with a zest unparalleled. Mardi Gras is a carnival unlike any other in the United States, and the Jazz and Heritage Festival each spring is not far behind. Add to that the debauch of St. Patrick's Day and the celebratory atmosphere of Sugar and Super Bowls, and, when hurricanes hit, some people don't leave; they have a hurricane party. "You can make a good reputation for yourself in this town as an efficient businessman just by returning phone calls," one musician told me.

It was this party-time industry that brought me and the Judge and the Stripper here years ago, and it was this same atmosphere that I had to fight in my quest for the blues.

I left my hotel in the Garden District and took a streetcar named St. Charles to the French Quarter. It was early for New Orleans—about eleven in the morning—so I stopped in at Café Du Monde for café au lait, made with chicory coffee and hot milk, and *beignets*—square, deepfried donuts. Let other people spend their life savings eating at Brennen's. This is a real New Orleans breakfast. You can sit and watch the daily carnival of the Quarter go by.

After about three cups of coffee, I wandered over to North Rampart Street and what's left of Congo Square. Now called Louis Armstrong Park, Congo Square is where the slaves used to dance on Sundays; it's where Buddy Bolden, the mysterious trumpet player, is said to have first played jazz. You can look across the park and see the housing project on Basin Street—low brick buildings squatting on the same ground that once supported the palatial brothels of Storyville. There are only a few winos in the park now, sprawled on benches, and a cop or two who walk slowly through the area. The place is filled only with ghosts of the music.

I left the park, lightly touching the giant statue of Armstrong as I passed, and walked down St. Ann Street, once the home of Marie Laveau, the city's most famous voodoo queen. The dark specter of voodoo hangs over New Orleans. The religion supposedly came from Africa by way of Haiti. In New Orleans it became a part of the black culture. Marie Laveau and its other leaders may have stayed in New Orleans but voodoo or hoodoo traveled up the Mississippi and throughout the South. Yet on St. Ann Street, only a small plaque tells that the great Marie Laveau once lived there. Ghosts.

I walked over to Dumaine Street to see the New Orleans Historic Voodoo Museum. Inside, a woman dressed like Elvira, Queen of the Night, a television hostess of horror movies, stood behind a wooden counter ministering to the needs of tourists.

"Excuse me," I said, "I wonder if you've got a nice mojo hand I could buy?" A mojo hand is a root that looks like a paw and it's a standard good-luck charm mentioned in blues lyrics.

"Gosh, honey, I'm sorry," said the Elvira clone, "I'm fresh out of mojo hands. But I expect some any day now. Is there something else I can help you with?"

I remembered the lyrics of "Hoochie-Coochie Man."

"Yeah. I'll take a black cat bone and a John-the-Conqueror Root."

"All right," she said, smiling like an apothecary clerk from hell, "one black-cat bone and a John-the-Conqueror root. Now we have a variety of black-cat bones," she said as she took them from a shelf behind her and displayed them on the counter, each in a small clear-plastic box. "They start at fifteen dollars." I noticed a small card pinned to each black-cat bone. It read, NOVELTY ITEM. SOLD FOR AMUSEMENT ONLY.

She pulled a small ladder up behind her and climbed to reach a jar on the top shelf. Inside it was a large, brown, phallic tuber.

"Did you want the whole root or just a small part of it? I can cut off any size you need. By the way, just what is it you're trying to do with this stuff?"

"Ah, I'm trying to be a hoochie-coochie man."

"Umm-huum. Well, the John-the-Conquerer Root is twenty-five dollars."

"Forget it," I said as I turned to walk out, "penicillin's cheaper."

On my way back, I turned down Bourbon Street. If the Stripper were still in town, still working, this is where she'd be. Women's Lib has come to New Orleans, I noticed, as I walked down the street which seemed to have been taken over by a band of T-shirt merchants: there are as many bars offering male strippers as female. I stopped and looked at a shirt that read, PINCH ME, PEEL ME, EAT ME . . . LOUISIANA CRAYFISH and then walked into the Showbar, perched on a bar stool, and ordered a beer. Onstage were a couple of tired, middle-aged naked women, bumping and grinding to the blues. They wore only pasties and expressions of resignation as they turned and stared at themselves in the mirror behind the bar. If one of them was the stripper I'd come to town with years before, I didn't want to know.

"Hi, hon," a woman behind me said. "Wanna buy me a drink?"

I turned to look. It was a woman in a negligée, young enough to be the Stripper's daughter.

"No thanks," I said and turned around.

"Goddamnit," she shouted, grabbing the hair on the back of my head, "I said buy me a drink."

"Listen," I said, shaking loose and getting up to leave, "I'm not into S and M."

"Queer," she shouted as I walked out the door, "lousy queer!"

It was getting dark now, and still no blues. But the day slips past in New Orleans and you're not aware of it. Maybe it's the heat. It could be the humidity. But whatever it is had a strong hold on me. I walked over to Arnaud's bar and ordered a drink. I suppose I should have asked for a cocktail since that word originated in New Orleans as a description of a mixture of brandy and Peychaud bitters served in an eggcup called a *coquetier*. The name of the eggcup was corrupted over the years to *cocktail*. Instead, I asked for a Sazerac. It used to be a mixture of whiskey and absinthe plus Peychaud bitters, but about the time Storyville was outlawed, so was absinthe. Today they use Herbsaint, a Pernod-like, licorice liqueur. When I left the bar, the town had a glow that hadn't been there before.

I walked over to Felix's for a couple of dozen oysters and then back down Bourbon toward a club in the 600 block called Bourbon Street After Hours. An old bluesman named Ironing Board Sam was supposed to be playing there.

I found the place, and there was a tiny stage in one corner behind the bar. But there was no Ironing Board Sam. Instead, a one-man band playing Johnny Cash songs was onstage. I ordered a drink and listened to the third chorus of "I Walk the Line." When the band left to less than thunderous applause, I asked the bartender about Sam.

"Oh, Lord, honey," she said. "He's not here. He used to play here all the time, you know, but he went to England and found Jesus. I guess he don't play the blues no more."

I told her I wasn't in the mood for Johnny Cash. She said she understood, neither was she, but what could she do about it?

I wandered around a little more, avoiding the barkers at the strip joints. Once the strippers had been great stars like Lilly St. Cyr, Evelyn West, and a woman named Tee-Tee Red who balanced champagne glasses on her breasts and then drank out of them without using her hands.

From outside the Old Absinthe House I hailed a White Fleet cab. I'd heard about a brass band called The Dirty Dozen who mixed traditional New Orleans jazz, be-bop, and Caribbean rhythms. They played at midnight at The Glass House on Saratoga and Second. I got in the cab and we started off.

"Where to?" Driver Number 149 asked.

"Saratoga and Second," I told him.

He slammed on his brakes. "Say what?"

"Saratoga and Second, a bar called The Glass House. It's a couple of blocks off South Rampart."

"Mister, you don't want to go there."

"Why not?"

"It's a bad neighborhood, Mister. Real bad."

"But they've got a band called The Dirty Dozen that's

playing there tonight. They're famous. They've been on Johnny Carson."

"Mister, there's lots of bands here in the Quarter. Why don't you go see one of them. They probably just as good."

I told him I wanted to go to The Glass House and if he didn't take me, I'd find a driver who would. He sighed, shifted into gear, and we drove off. Saratoga and Second is in the midst of the ghetto. The streets are dark and the old wooden buildings look sinister in the moonlight. We turned down Saratoga, a narrow street that looked no wider than an alley. Ahead there was a lighted, plastic Miller beer sign. In small letters beneath the beer logo it said, THE GLASS HOUSE.

"This is it, I guess," I said.

"Yeah. You get out and run to the door," the driver said. "Get in as quick as you can. I got a pistol in the car. I'll keep you covered."

He was reaching for the glove compartment as I scurried the few feet to the door. It was locked. I knocked. The driver of the cab was keeping a close lookout. Someone came to the door, unlocked it, and opened it a crack.

"Dirty Dozen playing here tonight?" I asked.

"Yeah," the man answered. I walked back to the cab and paid the driver.

"Better than I thought," the cabbie said. "They keep the door locked. That's good. Less trouble that way. You probably all right once you're inside."

It was a small club, five or six tables and a bar. It would seat maybe thirty people. But Thelma, who owns the place and was working behind the bar, assured me that on most nights when The Dirty Dozen played there as many as a hundred people jammed into the small, wooden building. She was right. An hour or so later, when the band arrived, the place was packed. People were sitting on the floor, leaned against the walls, and outside there was a line waiting to get in.

The Dirty Dozen is a brass band and, while they play traditional New Orleans music, they mix it with Thelonious Monk, television cartoon themes, and the "Star-Spangled Banner." The music is so infectious, you cannot sit still while they play. With bands like this, it's no wonder New Orleans has so many parades. Until I heard The Dirty Dozen, I thought New Orleans brass bands were a relic, something they hauled out for tourists and conventioneers. But this music was as up-to-date as Michael Jackson and at the same time, as traditional as Buddy Bolden.

After the band had played for an hour or so nonstop, trumpets blaring, the big sound of a Sousaphone keeping the bass rhythms and two trombones adding fizz, they took a break and I managed to talk with Gregory Davis, one of two trumpet players with the group. I told him I was surprised to see such a packed house, since my cab driver was afraid to come into the neighborhood.

"Yeah, this neighborhood can be pretty rough and, you know, this club has had a rough tradition, a rough history. A lot of the cab drivers, they don't know it's OK to come here. This area, the neighborhood itself, there are many times I wouldn't come up here because of the reputation it's had in the past. But it's not like that anymore."

We talked for a while about his musical background and the band's history.

"I got started in music by accident myself. I had an older brother who was going to summer music camp. I wasn't old enough to go. And he enrolled in this music class and he would bring the horn home. It was a baritone. But he was more interested in baseball and basketball and that sort of stuff. And when he would leave, I would practice on his horn. I guess I was about eleven years old then.

"Most of us in the band got our beginning with the Danny Barker youth program that he had going with the Fairview Baptist Band. It was a brass band being run by Danny Barker, who is an old-time musician here, you know. He was concerned that not many of the young people were getting involved with New Orleans music. This was like in 1973 or 1974. And he took a lot of heat from the other musicians, older musicians. He was accused of trying to take gigs away from the older musicians. At that time I think I was about fourteen or something like that. But that's not what was going on at all. He was just trying to get a band started that would have some young people in it.

"When we started, there were just old men playing in the brass bands. That was in the summer of 1977. At that time, I was twenty-one and there wasn't anywhere to play if you wanted to be in a brass band. Just rock and roll was happening. Oh, there were the older brass bands—Onward, Tuxedo, and Olympia—and you'd get hired every now and then, but it wasn't anything you could count on. So we just started rehearsing together. Not with the intention of being radical or anything like that—just rehearsing to try to learn some music.

"And, lo and behold, once people knew there was another band available, we started getting jobs, because the older bands didn't do parades anymore, or the softball games, or the picnics. Every now and then they did a funeral, but not much. They would turn out only for the funeral of another musician. We started getting so much work that sometimes I had to put together a second band just to use the Dirty Dozen name. And we worked six nights a week, sometimes two and three gigs a day. That went on for about two years straight. And then some other guys started realizing we couldn't get all the work and so other bands started popping up, like the Rebirth Jazz Band at the Chosen Few. So now, today, I'd say there are about twenty brass bands working in the city," Davis said.

"See, in New Orleans, there are these social and pleasure clubs. For a lot of them, their main function is just to raise a lot of money to have a big parade and parties and dances. Most of 'em have an annual event day when they have their parade. This is separate from Mardi Gras. They buy these elaborate costumes. You gotta see it. But when we started, all the social and pleasure club parades no longer existed. There just wasn't anybody to play them or the softball games or the dances or the picnics or the weddings and that sort of stuff.

"Most of the guys in the band had spent years in rock and roll. But in a rock band you wait around for ten minutes and play two notes. And after those two notes you wait around another ten minutes, just standing there dancing. And so we were searching for a way to play more, and brass bands were a way.

"I guess we got some encouragement when we started, but we got more *dis*couragement. And a lot of it came from the older guys because we were playing the music a whole lot different—the rhythm, anyway—from what they were used to hearing.

"The objections were to some of the songs we were

playing. Like, we tried "Night Train" at a funeral or in one of the parades. Or "Caravan" or "Bongo Beat." So the older guys said we were not sticking to the traditions. Well, we knew that. But we weren't saying, 'Let's do something to break the tradition.' It was a situation where we were rehearsing five or six nights a week and not getting any traditional gigs anyhow. So we started all this other stuff. When we got a gig, we'd play as much traditional stuff as we had ready. But then when it was time to play another song, well, hey, we rehearsed this, let's try it. So we got a lot of flak about that. But. man, I get tired of playing 'When the Saints Go Marchin' In.' That song is so requested. I mean, as long as you don't play it more than once or twice a day it's OK. But that and 'Bourbon Street Parade,' all over Europe, Japan, and South America, that's what they want to hear.

"We started playing here at The Glass House because there was a parade one Sunday afternoon and Thelma—the woman that owns the place—her boyfriend asked us when the parade was over to come play here. The parade was over like at five or six o'clock, something like that. And we played until ten o'clock that night. Well, by eight or nine they had sold everything drinkable in the place. I mean there was nothing left. Not even ice. Then the next weekend we tried it again and there were just about the same results. From that point on, we played on Monday because a lot of the clubs have their dinner on the Monday following the parades. So we just became expected to be here on Monday nights.

"So, then, well, you know about the jazz festival here every year, right? Well, George Wein is the producer of that. Anyway, some people who knew of the band thought we should play there and at some other festivals they produce around the country and in Europe. I remember the day he came to see us. We were playing at an elementary school, McDonald Forty-two, and they were having their annual children's fair, or something like that. And the band was set up and playing in this treehouse out on the playground. He liked us, I guess, because we got on the festival and now we've played all over the country and at festivals in Europe. We recorded then, first on Concord and then for Rounder," Davis said.

"For a while there, New Orleans music was on the way out. Back when I was twelve or thirteen and started playing in a rhythm-and-blues band, there must have been hundreds of bands like ours all over the place. And then around the time disco came through, it just wiped out a whole generation of instrumental musicians. Now, with no places to perform, instead of the kids wanting to play in a band after school or do some kind of music at night, they were getting jobs at the Burger King or McDonald's and at the supermarkets.

"Rhythm and blues is doing better, now that disco is on the way out, but a lot of clubs still don't hire bands. There are more groups than there were five years ago but nothing like ten or fifteen years ago. When the clubs stopped hiring bands and started hiring deejays, that just wiped it out. But, you know, the bands that are playing, it's not really a New Orleans sound. Now the bands are imitating whatever is in the Top Forty. And it really is a shame because New Orleans did have its own distinctive rhythm-and-blues sound.

"As you know, there's very few blues bands around here, and I don't know why. A lot of the barrooms have jukeboxes with hundred of blues records on them and a lot of older people, in their thirties and forties, really do like to listen to the blues. What it all boils down to is if I did start a blues band, where would I play? I mean, Bourbon Street is almost a joke. A lot of the clubs have turned into auction houses where they have people bid on these radios and appliances and things. And then, man, everything else down there almost is a T-shirt shop. So many T-shirts and not much music."

Greg had to start playing again, and I called a cab and left. There were still people lined up outside as I rode off through the darkened streets. I went back to the French Quarter for a while, looked again for some blues, and had no luck. I decided to head back to the hotel.

As I walked down Bourbon to Canal to catch the streetcar, wisps of fog were settling over the city. While I waited I heard, from somewhere, the wail of a tenor saxophone. I looked, but couldn't see it. The music echoed off the buildings in the business district and swirled through the fog. No matter how hard I looked, I couldn't see who was playing it or where, but the phantom saxophone made me think of Buddy Bolden, Storyville, Congo Square, Marie Laveau, Louis Armstrong. The streetcar came and I got on. We drove away from the music. Ghosts.

The next morning I rode into the Quarter again, had two cups of coffee at Café du Monde, then walked over to the Pantalba Building at the corner of Jackson Square and St. Peter. The bar has French doors that open in warm weather, so it's almost like sitting on a patio. I nursed my hangover with a beer and watched the portrait artists set up on the square. They had a gimmick. Usually, they could draw a standard male face and a standard female face. A mark comes along to get a portrait painted. Put in the right color of hair and eyes, make a few distinguishing marks, and that's it. A portrait of your own self, made right on Jackson Square in the French Quarter. Enjoy your stay in New Orleans.

I lit a cigar, ordered another beer, and watched the tourists get suckered in by the artists. Then I noticed a man with a beard who apparently had some authority to clear the streets. As he did, someone rolled a movie camera out of a truck. Another man hauled out a microphone and a few klieg lights.

"What are they doing?" I asked my waitress.

"They're making an Italian movie," she said, obviously unimpressed. I watched for a while. Judging from the rehearsals, the scene called for a couple to sit on a park bench, talk for a minute, and then wander arm-in-arm up the street. It seemed easy enough, but they repeated it interminably. I was about to pay and leave when a brass band pulled up, got out of their car and began playing.

It wasn't The Dirty Dozen but another of the twenty or more groups that are part of the brass-band renaissance. The band played, the actors went through their paces and finally, even though it was for camera, I was getting a taste of New Orleans French Quarter music that transcended the hype on Bourbon Street. The music sounded like swinging bebop played in march time, like the blues written by John Philip Sousa, like a funky circus band awash with the rhythmic lappings of the Mississippi river.

I listened to the band for about an hour and then called Ben Sandmill. He'd been trying to set up a meeting between me and Snooks Eaglin. The problem, Sandmill told me, was that Snooks thought everybody was trying to make a buck at his expense. If he talked to anyone, he wanted to be paid for it. Say "five hundred dollars" and he'd talk. I wasn't surprised. In his book, *The Legacy of the Blues*, Sam Charters called Eaglin, "an elusive and difficult man, as unavailable to interviewers as he has been to record companies." Charters didn't get to talk to him either. But it wasn't all bad news. Canadian television was in town doing a film about Eaglin. That afternoon he was playing a set for the television cameras at a bar called Tyler's in the Garden District.

I stopped for an oyster loaf and a beer and thought about Snooks Eaglin. As Charters said, "To call Snooks a blues singer is over-romanticizing him." He plays some blues, but like most New Orleans musicians, the blues is only one element of what he does.

Eaglin was born in 1937, an apparently normal baby. When he was nineteen months old, he was found to have a brain tumor. An operation saved his life but left him blind. When he was six, he started playing the guitar. At twelve he won a radio talent contest playing "Twelfth Street Rag." After that he played a little here, a little there, and finally was recorded as a street singer that Folkways Records found on Bourbon Street hustling the tourists. He played the Playboy Club in New Orleans for a while, toured and recorded with Professor Longhair, but never seemed to hit the big time as a solo act. Finally, in the early 1970s, he played the New Orleans Jazz Festival and, as a result was booked at some festivals in Europe. But, like Charters says, he's elusive.

Inside Tyler's, technicians were adjusting lights and

microphones. Snooks was not there yet. Since I didn't have the money it took to talk to him, I had to settle for a free concert. Not bad. Snooks arrived and was led right to the bandstand. There was no talking, no asides, nothing. He was being paid to play and that's all he was going to do. Once he started, I realized that it was worth missing the interview just to see him perform. In his voice was the whole modern New Orleans tradition—Smiley Lewis, Fats Domino, Professor Longhair. In his playing there were the bouncy rhythms of the city, the thrill of carnival, the sense of place that is uniquely New Orleans.

He played for more than an hour—old Smiley Lewis tunes like "Down Yonder," his own compositions like "Don't Leave No News" and "That Same Old Train," classics like "A Teeny Bit of Your Love," "Let the Four Winds Blow," and "Mustang Sally." It was one of the most remarkable performances I'd seen. And then, too soon, it was over. Snooks was led from the stage, nodded once, and left. The Canadian television crew was left to interview the members of his band.

I left and went over to Frankie and Johnnie's for some crayfish. As I pinched them, peeled them and ate them, I thought about New Orleans. No wonder jazz was born here; no wonder the lonesome sound of the blues became sublimated. No wonder the food was beyond compare. America claims to be a melting pot but it's really not. Except in New Orleans. Like other Southern cities, there's been segregation and racial strife. Nevertheless, there is a unique blending of cultures. It's the only true melting pot in America. And from that pot comes the tastiest gumbo.

I rode back to my room at the St. Charles Inn, had

a nightcap, and went to bed. I dreamed about New Orleans. There were jazz bands, blues singers, Storyville
women, dancing, crayfish, second-liners, and a swirl of
voodoo queens. The Judge and the Stripper had cameos.
That, I suppose, is one of those dreamy dreams they sing
about.

5

IT TAKES A LITTLE more than two hours to drive from New Orleans to Lafayette, the capital of Cajun Louisiana. Most of the people who live here are descended from exiles. The Acadians were French settlers who came to Port Royal in Acadia, a part of Canada. Essentially, they were an isolated people, outside the mainstream of New France. The Colony often changed hands between the French and English, but in 1713, England gained permanent control of Acadia and renamed it Nova Scotia. Once the English were in command, the French colonists were exiled, many of them traveling all the way to Louisiana where they hoped to build a society like the one they had been forced to abandon in Canada.

In Louisiana, the Acadians reestablished their culture and absorbed other ethnic groups around them—French Creoles, Germans, Americans, and Afro-Caribbeans—to form a society called Cajun, which, of course, is a corruption of Acadian. Some of the Cajuns settled in isolation along the bayous; others moved to the Western Louisiana prairies. In the towns and on the farms of these prairies Cajun music developed.

It was a white music, dominated by accordions and fiddles. The accordions came from German settlers, the fiddles from Anglo-Saxons. When black Cajuns first played the music, it was not much different from what the small white bands were playing—country dances called the *fais dodo* and waltzes. But over the years black music and white music went in different directions, the white bands sounding more country and western and the black groups incorporating the blues. Initially, the black music was called La-la, and some old people still call it that. But gradually, it became known as zydeco, a shortened corruption of the French phrase, *"les haricots ne sont pas salés,"* which translates as "the snapbeans are not salty."

"La-la was a house dance when thirty, forty, fifty people got together to have a good time," according to an interview with Clarence Gallien, an old-time zydeco musician, in *Meeting the Blues* by Alan Govenar. "The name changed from la-la to zydeco when Clifton Chenier made the record, 'Les Haricots Son Pas Salé.' "

There had been other black cajun performers before Chenier, of course—people like Aiphonse "Bois Sec" Ardoin and Boozoo Chavis—but Clifton Chenier, the undisputed "King of Zydeco," gave the music its present form back in the 1950s. He was to zydeco what Bill Monroe was to bluegrass.

"When I was small, there was a lot of them around playing accordion," Chenier said in an interview years ago with Alan Govenar in *Meeting the Blues.*

> Zydeco was strong in '43, '44, with the old people, way back. But it faded out. They'd zydeco in the houses in the old times, with the violin, accordion, and rub-board. No drums. They just stopped it. I brought it back. I keep that French in there but I got a little rock in it, too. A lot of people used to laugh at me. They'd say the accordion couldn't

make it, but then I had a hit in 1955 and that got them. They opened their eyes. I was way ahead of them.

I used to listen to B. B. King, Fats Domino, things like that when I was learning. I listened to Fats a whole lot and all those New Orleans piano players. Professor Longhair was one of 'em. The beat came from the religion people.

I never picked up an accordion until 1947 after my uncle got me one. I learned how to play boogie on the accordion. People didn't understand how the accordion could make those sounds. What I did was my own thing. Nobody showed me.

Perhaps nobody had ever heard the blues from an accordion before because the traditional Cajun instrument is a four-stop button model. Chenier used an accordion with a piano keyboard which could make blue notes that were impossible on the simpler one. He also changed the washboard from a hand-held utilitarian instrument to a corrugated metal breast plate, worn around the neck. It was played originally by his brother, Cleveland Chenier. The washboard adds a staccato rhythm, making it almost impossible to sit still when you hear the music.

I hoped to talk to Chenier when I got to Lafayette, but I'd been warned it would be almost impossible. He has diabetes and parts of both feet have been amputated. He doesn't talk to much of anybody he doesn't know.

In Lafayette, I stopped by the house where Shelton Skarrett lived. Skarrett was recording the Sams Brothers Five, a zydeco equivalent of the Jackson Five, and had invited me to come to the session. The studio was a converted garage at Skarrett's house. More properly, it was his parent's house. Skarrett's in his early twenties and still lives at home. Although on their early records there is a deep funk overtone to the Sams Brothers music, it still sounds like zydeco, complete with washboard, percussion, and accordion. The Sams Brothers are the sons of Good Rockin' Herbert Sam, who is directing the session. The boys started playing in the 1970s when they were little and cute, but their talent exceeded the novelty of seeing five prepubescent boys playing the blues, so they have continued.

That day there were a couple of problems. One of the keys on Leon Sam's accordion was sticking, and Skarrett's father was due home soon.

Nobody said so, but it was apparent that Daddy Skarrett didn't allow any zydeco music in here. Skarrett's mother called him into the kitchen for a minute and when he came out, he said he'd have to wrap the session up for the day. He didn't say Daddy's coming home, but it was easy to guess.

Once the session broke up, I left and headed over to see Rockin' Dopsie, who billed himself as the Crowned Prince of Zydeco. Dopsie got himself crowned a couple of years back at a ceremony in Lafayette. Clifton Chenier is the King of Zydeco and usually appears in publicity pictures wearing a crown. But Dopsie was not to be outdone. He bought his own crown and invented a new title.

On the way over, I stopped at a pay phone and called Clifton Chenier. A woman answered the phone. She was vague about an interview, but suggested I call back.

Dopsie lives in a middle-class Lafayette subdivision. His home is a brick rancher and if there is a blues life reflected in his music, it comes from earlier days. His home

and the ones surrounding it look like an ideal neighborhood for insurance adjusters. Dopsie is a round, friendly
man with a thick French accent. We sat in comfortable
leather chairs in his den and drank Jack Daniels from a
decanter that played "How Dry I Am" every time you
picked it up.

"Well, zydeco music is very strong right now," he said
as he took a sip of the whiskey. "It's picked up in the last
three or four years like wild grass. Now I first started out
in the music thirty-three years ago. So I'm almost an old
root. 'Course, I was just playing locally then. The zydeco
wasn't spread around the whole world like it is now. I
remember I met Clifton in 1955. Me and him gave a few
shows together, a few jam sessions. At that time, I do believe that me and Clifton were the only two who was really
playing. Oh, there may have been some more but, you
know we was the only two really making it. He was older
than me and had been on the road and had lots more
experience. So one night Clifton heard me play. I was
playing at a club on Breaux Bridge Road called Roger's
Night Club. Clifton told me we needed to get together.
He said he liked my style, said he'd been all over and never
met nobody like me. We got together about two weeks
later. It was on Monday at a club called the Blue Angel
and we did a jam session there, me and him. And he told
me, 'You're gonna be great, man, you're the only musician
who can stick with me like that.' Now, when I did that with
Clifton, I already had a following. But after that, I got
even bigger audiences. People heard me playing with Clifton and they knew I could play real good. That was when
he was a young man and had all his power. Clifton, he was
all right.

"At that time, I was working construction during the

day and playing music at night. I was playing seven nights a week. That time there, those joints and saloons could stay open twenty-four hours a day. Long as you wanted. There was always something going on. Back then, I was working eight hours a day with a shovel, but I was really interested in my music. I kept thinking, man, I hope I can get enough money so I can give up this construction job. But I was only making fifty dollars a night, and I had to pay three guys out of that. You couldn't live on that shit.

"It took me fifteen years of working construction and playing music at night before my goal struck. And when it struck, man, I just put the shovel down. It was in 1976, I think, when I met this guy from Stockholm, Sweden. His name was Sam Charters and he was a producer for the Sonet Record Company. Sam heard me at the jazz festival in New Orleans. So, after the show, he came by my house. And he said, man, I really like the way you play. I'd like to do some recording with you. Naturally, I say, yeah. Then on Monday morning he shows up and signed me up for a three-year contract. Tuesday we went into the studio and boom! Here's an album. Three months later the album comes out and he gives me another call. He wondered if I'd like to tour around Europe. Oh, I was so excited. It looked like the biggest thing in my whole life. When I got back from Europe, I didn't know what I was gonna do about my job. But I was working for a good man and he said whenever I come back my job was there. So I went back on my job and worked construction for a couple of weeks again and then they call me to go back to Europe. Well, I gave up the job and I kept the music.

"You know, I'm from a little town near Lafayette, a town called Carencro—about six miles outside of Lafayette. My father played accordion, but it was like a French accordion, a little squeeze box. I always did admire the accordion and I told my mother than when I got big enough I was gonna buy one. They used to always have them country-house dances on weekends, and they called the music they played la-la music. I used to go with my mother and, believe me, it was fun," Dopsie said.

"Then when I got to be about twelve years old, they bought me an accordion. It didn't take me no time to learn. At the end of two or three weeks I was playing songs. But it didn't have enough keys on it for me. So they gave me a bigger one for Christmas. Back then, the music sounded more like French. It was a lot of those Cajun bands playing French music. There wasn't too many black people playing zydeco. You know, when zydeco first got started, it was just a washboard and an accordion. That's really zydeco. That's all they had. They didn't have no drums, no guitars, no horns, no nothing. Just a washboard and an accordion. And, boy, that really sounds good to me. When I got started it was just me and another guy on washboard. And I did that for fourteen years. I did more work then when it was just us two than I do now with this big bunch of guys I got playing for me."

The decanter played its tune as we poured another drink. I asked Dopsie about Rockin' Sidney, the only person who's had a big hit with a zydeco tune, "My Toot-Toot."

"Sydney's an amateur compared to me. He's not really zydeco. I call that disco zydeco. Every little band that comes up now, they call themselves zydeco. But it's disco, man. Well, to be honest with you, if you want to play zydeco, you've got to be French. Because zydeco is French music. If you're not French, I don't know how you could do it. I never heard no Englishman who could play it. Of course,

Paul Simon, he's all right. I was on his album, "Graceland."
So Paul's all right. But he's a little French, I believe. But
in zydeco, I do believe I'm the biggest star that ever was
born. My sons play it, too. The one in the band who plays
the washboard, that's my son. And the drummer, Alton,
that's my oldest son."

He rummaged through a stack of clippings. "This here
is when they crowned me the Prince of Zydeco. I'm the
prince. Clifton's the king. But he's just barely hanging in
there now, poor thing.

"I don't think I could tell you much about the younger
bands around here. They're not playing zydeco. We've had
a get-together with the Sams Brothers, but they're not playing zydeco. Now Boozoo Chavis out of Lake Charles, he
play nice. You got Queen Ida in San Francisco. She calls
herself zydeco, but her music is more Spanish, not French.
Now, blues is a big part of zydeco and I love the blues.
But there's one promise I made myself, that I'd never
change the style of my music. Because this is the old-culture
music.

"You know, me and my wife, we still speak French
around the house. She's French too, from up around
Breaux Bridge. But now they've started to teach French
in the schools. It used to be I could tell my wife something
in French, the kids wouldn't know what it means. Now we
speak in French and they repeat back to me in English
what I just said.

"You know, zydeco, it's a party music, if you want to
be frank about it. That's what it's all about. You want to
take your wife out for a good time, go to zydeco. It works
better if I can play where people dance. Everywhere I go
people be dancing, even if it's in the mud. It's that beat—
man it makes people dance with no legs at all. There's a

man at a club called Slim's Y-Ki-Ki. He's in a wheelchair. No legs. When I'm playin', that man be jumping up and down in his chair. That chair be spinning a hundred miles an hour. There's a lady that come out and catch his hand and they go spinnin' off. Yeah!"

I left Dopsie's in search of live music. And on the weekend, there's a lot to choose from. The only difficulty is the mileage between bars. There's Gretta's Turf and Mary's Country Club in St. Martinsville, small clubs that feature hot zydeco bands. But the most famous place is thirty miles up the road in Opelousas—Slim's Y-Ki-Ki. The bar is famous because Rockin' Sidney, the man who made a hit out of "My Toot-Toot," sings about the place on a couple of albums.

The Y-Ki-Ki Club is a concrete-block building on the outskirts of Opelousas. There's no big neon sign. Souvenir T-shirts are not available. Inside, there's Jax Beer on tap and a local band on the stand. The local group, it turns out, is Clifton Chenier's son C. J. and his father's Red Hot Louisiana band. C. J. plays saxophone, but even with the addition of brass, the presence of accordion and wash-board keep the music well within the parameters of zydeco. A few palm trees are painted on the wall behind the band. The place has been open thirty years and it's not a club, really. Like every other place in this Cajun land, it's a dance hall. Few couples have taken the floor because a lone dancer is shuffling to the band's rhythms and he cuts a broad path between tables. Finally, seeing that much of her crowd is intimidated, a woman named Irene, the owner of the club, comes out from behind the bar and grabs the man and lectures him.

"What do you mean acting like this?" she says. "Why

are you acting like this? Don't you see there are other people here who want to have fun? You listen to me now, I could throw your ass out of here. Right now. You go sit down. And don't you do this again. I'm gonna be watching, and if you do, I'm throwing you out. You understand?"

The man said he did, and as he sat sheepishly in the corner, people started dancing. Most of the customers were black, but there was one white couple sitting at a table near the rear, sipping beer and listening to the music.

I had a couple of beers and listened to C. J. Chenier. The traditional elements of zydeco were there—the accordion and the Caribbean rhythms of the washboard, but it was the addition of a saxophone that gave it a more urban, rhythm-and-blues feeling. When the band took a break, I talked to C. J. for a while. If I couldn't talk to the King of Zydeco himself, at least I could chat with his son.

"To tell you the truth, it makes me real proud to know that my dad almost invented zydeco," C. J. said. "You can't say that about too many people. I wouldn't really say he invented it, but he surely revised it and brought it to where it is today. He made everybody take notice of it.

"You see, I didn't grow up here in Louisiana with my father. I grew up in Port Arthur, Texas, with my mother. My father was always on the road, so I only saw him two or three times a year. I started playing saxophone after my mother bought one for me and then I played it in the school band. I took piano lessons for a couple of months and then my daddy bought me a guitar.

"My father's always been reluctant to give interviews because, through the years, some of the hard things he went through made him take the attitude that people was trying to use him. A lot of people brought him through a lot of changes. He got kinda paranoid about that and has gotten to the point where he'd just rather not talk to any-body because he's afraid of being used. Back then, when he was starting out, it was much harder on a musician and he wasn't as protected as he is now. Especially him. He just came through the school of hard knocks.

"A lot of people keep calling this music Cajun, but zydeco and Cajun is two completely different things. Zy-deco is much bluesier and Cajun has got a lot of fiddle in it and, basically, just sort of a one-two beat. Zydeco is more upbeat, soulful. What can I say? A zydeco dance has got shuffles, waltzes, all that—it's not Cajun at all.

"I just moved to Lafayette from Port Arthur, which is about a hundred-twenty miles from Louisiana. It used to be the other way. People moved from Louisiana to Texas to work in the oil fields. But there's nothing going on in Port Arthur now, nothing at all. That's what happens to a place when they depend on one resource. They didn't have nothing to fall back on. Now they don't have no music, nothing. After the oil crunch, that was it for Port Arthur.

"You know, I didn't start out playing zydeco. The first band I ever played with was funk—a Top-Forty band. I was sixteen years old. But I been playing zydeco since seventy-eight. Like, one week before I made twenty-one, I started playing zydeco. My dad called up and wanted me to play with him. I wasn't doing nothing, I didn't have a job, so I said OK. I mean, I was still playing with that little Top-Forty band, but that was all local. I made two records with Clifton Chenier that we went in the studio to do, but there's been other bootleg stuff coming out, stuff made at live performances that I didn't know about.

"You know, I think the new interest in zydeco has come about because of Clifton Chenier's strong will to go out there and push with all that power of his. Once he gets onstage, there wasn't anything else going on. It all came after he showed it could be done, after he imposed his will on people. There wasn't really anybody else at that time who was really big in this music, you know. Oh, there was Rockin' Dopsie and Fernest Arceneaux, they were around but they were just playing around Lafayette, not touring or anything.

"Of course, zydeco goes way back. My daddy talks about how they used to have house parties when they didn't have clubs. They didn't have guitars or amplification—just him and a drummer and a washboard. They played and people would party all night long.

"Now, with my music, I don't try to make it too different from him by much. But with me not being him, I mean of course it's different. As you know, he's the great Clifton Chenier and there can't be another one of him. But if I sound like anybody, it'd be him because he's the only one I ever listen to. My music, I guess you could say, is a little more citified. Because I'm not really trying to imitate him, I'm trying to establish myself. I'm not gonna sit down and try to learn his stuff note-for-note. I'm just gonna go for it the way I feel.

"I really didn't spend any time in Layfayette until now. I used to get teased in school, but the kids didn't know what was happenin'. They used to say, 'Your daddy plays chinky-chink music,' stuff like that. They called it la-la music. I didn't know until I started traveling with him how the people responded to his music. I just knew I liked it, even if, at that time, I didn't know one song from another.

"We get along pretty well together. We've been touring together for ten years. My mama says we're kinda alike. Sometimes he doesn't like something I like, but for the most part, we get along. Some people say he's hard to get along with but it depends on who you are. He's a sick person, you know, bad sick. And it depends on how he feels that day. Sometimes when he's feeling good he gets along with the world. Other times he's feeling bad and just doesn't want to be bothered.

"Zydeco is what he's all about. He's never even talked about playing in other kinds of bands because he is strictly about accordions and zydeco. Matter of fact, he told me I didn't need nothing. Didn't need a saxophone. Didn't need college. All I needed was an accordion. That's what he's about. Nothing else has ever entered his mind. You know, he started recording in 1955 and here it is twenty years or more later and he's just catching on. Maybe people used to laugh at him, but when he started driving around in Cadillacs, they quit laughin' and started listening."

The next morning I drove over to Eunice to talk to Mark Savoy at his accordion factory. The sign out front says SAVOY MUSIC CENTER. In addition to the instruments he makes, Savoy sells sheet music, records, and a book about Cajun music written by his wife. I was too late for the Saturday morning jam session, but in time to talk to Savoy before he closed for the day.

Savoy is a big man with dark hair. He seems amiable enough, but I'd hate to be around him when he's mad. As he worked on a broken accordion, he talked about music and his life in the small, Louisiana town.

"It's so good living in a small town like this where everybody knows one another. I saw something the other day that really impressed me. I went to the bank that I do business with and this guy came in to cash his personal check. And he said, 'Dadgumit, I forgot my checkbook.' He needed twenty-five dollars. So the teller, she said,

'Here's twenty-five dollars, when you come back next time bring your checkbook.' Where would you find that? Then on Friday afternoon at the bank, it's the craziest thing— they've got popcorn in the back lounge and they've got beer and cocktails. Go in, help yourself to the beer, to a cocktail—and the popcorn's hot.

"There's so much music around here. Everywhere you go it's music, music, music. Several years ago a man asked me to do a little survey on accordion players. He said, 'Write down all the accordion players that you know in the city of Eunice.' When it got to two hundred, I stopped. There are just too many people in Eunice who play the accordion. And he just couldn't believe it. I'm not talking about people who play a dance every Saturday night, but people who have an accordion in their home and play music.

"You know, many years ago, I used to tell my poor mother, I said, 'One of these days the accordion's gonna get to be a very, very popular instrument.' And damned if it ain't happening. I mean, look at Cajun music, look at Tex-Mex, look at zydeco. Even the Irish thing. It's all happening and it all involves an accordion. One day the diatonic accordion might become as popular as an electric guitar.

"There's a guy from Houston who was asking me a question. He asked me to define zydeco. I said, 'Well, I'm not too good with words. I can tell you what it isn't. It's not some little white honky playing rock and roll and screaming zydeco, zydeco, zydeco every three or four seconds. And it ain't also some black jive-ass playing "Soul Train" on a keyboard accordion.' So I said, 'You take it from there. That's the way I see it.' Some of these white kids who try to sit in and play zydeco, it ain't Cajun, it's rock and roll, that's what it is. I tell you what I believe. I believe you can't play zydeco unless you're black. That's what I believe. Some of the 'zydeco' that I've heard some of these white guys playing, they better go back and listen to Clifton or Dopsie. They better do their homework.

"I heard people say this region's remained culturally pure because of isolation. They say the swamps acted as a barrier the same way the Appalachian Mountains acted as a barrier for hillbilly music. I don't know if that makes much sense, because we weren't isolated all that much. Ever since the late 1800s there was a lot of going back and forth to New Orleans. Even before the Acadians arrived here, there were settlers here. There were lots of French families, Italian families. And I believe all this area was settled way before. For instance, my ancestors came here from Italy way before the Acadians arrived, in 1699. The Acadians didn't just take a chance. They knew there was rich farmland here. I think it's the people themselves. You know, the Cajun people never made a big deal about nothing. Well, here we got this food, here we got this music, but they never made a big deal about themselves.

"The way I see the world, unless you make a big deal about something, it goes right over people's heads. They're so used to seeing the bag and not what's inside. In other words, if it's not marketed, nobody's gonna notice it. I think the Cajun attitude—just roll on, merrily we roll along—is why they never made a big deal about it. It's not because of the isolation, it's because of who they were," Savoy said.

"But for a traveler just coming through, a lot of people might not understand that this is a very unique part of the world. That we speak a foreign language and we play a different music. Somebody coming through, stopping at the McDonald's or at the Best Western Motels is not gonna discover our way of life. For that you go to the back roads. And lots of people traveling across the country never get off the Interstate. But that's changing. Because more and more people are tired of their American hot dogs. They're saying, 'Let's see if we find us a bowl of gumbo somewhere.'

"My accordion isn't that much different from the ones made by the forty other people in this country who make them. We all pattern our accordions on the same style—the same height, weight, general appearance. But there are degrees of difference just as there is between the cars you drive or the wine you drink. But if you're not a wine connoisseur, how can you know a good bottle of wine? Well, if you're not a good fiddler, how can you make a good fiddle? So there's a lot of these people who've picked up the craft that started sort of bass-ackwards. Instead of trying to learn the instrument and once they get good realizing that there's something missing and trying to figure what that certain elusive thing is, a lot of these people don't even play a note. So how can they know?

"Clifton's the one who wrote the book on zydeco. He pretty much set the standards of what zydeco should be. He's almost like the godfather. I remember overhearing a man say, 'Hey, Cliff, you better get ahold of yourself and start feeling better because if you go and die on us we ain't gonna have nothing new to play.' I mean, here's the old man waiting for Clifton to come out with a new composition so he can have something new to play. What a genius of a musician.

"I got into the accordion business because I started playing the music when I was twelve. All I had was the little pre-World War Two accordion. I was twelve years old—my father bought me one of these things. When I got that one it was twenty-seven-fifty. Now it costs two hundred dollars. But I knew there was something wrong, I knew there could be something better. I heard there was a man in Lake Charles who was making accordions. He was making copies of the prewar accordions. So, he was saying I'm gonna make a Rolls-Royce but I'm gonna use the parts of a Ford.

"I didn't think that was the right approach. So I began saying to myself, *What are the weak points here and how can I improve the instrument?* Of course, the weak points are the reeds. So I sent about two hundred letters out all over the world asking where can I buy a diatonic reed. I got one answer. I found a company that said, 'We can make genuine handmade Swedish steel reeds, the finest money can buy.' And it was the truth, too. And that's what I use.

"The minute these things can be mass-produced, it's gonna put us out of business. Whatever happened happens for the best. Outside interest is what kept this thing alive. If you would have come down here fifteen or twenty years ago, you would have seen a real difference. But what accounts for this new interest is people who want to find out what they are. I'm forty-six years old and ever since I was a boy I knew Cajun culture was something fantastic. I never went to one football game in my life. Instead of going to football games I would go to someone's house and say, 'Hey, play me a song, tell me a story.' I didn't have time to go to my high school graduation prom. I went to hear some old guys play some music. When I was a kid, I didn't even want to go out and play with my toys.

"You may walk into some little off-the-wall club somewhere down here and hear the best musicians. There's a lot of black people around here who play the single note accordion and play Cajun music. Zydeco is black Cajun blues. You know the black people have always, always,

always played their music different. Just like when black people make gumbo. It ain't the same as white people's gumbo. I remember when I was a kid and my father was a farmer. He had some tenant farmers and there was this old black woman who was living on the place. And she made the best cake I'd ever eaten. My mother was also a good baker but her cakes were nowhere the same as the ones from this old lady. Blacks have a different way of cooking, a different way of talking—their French is not the same. So of course their music is different.

"I remember my father telling me back in the days when he was a kid he remembered this old black man. He played the accordion. But that music was not like ours. Even though he played the same tune. It was like that old lady. She would use the same flour, the same eggs, the same butter, but her cake didn't taste like Mama's," Savoy said.

"You know, there's a Rip Van Winkle syndrome around here. People have been sleeping for so many years and have been disconnected from their culture. Some of these people don't even speak French. And their excuse is that Mama and Daddy never taught me how. Well, Mama and Daddy never taught me either. And so maybe one day these people will wake up and be proud they're Cajun. These people have been put down all their life. If there had been somebody around here to say, 'Do not give up your gumbo to chase after the American hot dog,' that would have been fine. But nobody done that with these people. What they did is say, 'You are nothing, you are nobody, you're not supposed to speak French. You're low class. I'm gonna whip you on the schoolyard if I catch you speaking French'—which is what happened, you know. So if all your life this culture meant bad, then of course you want to give it up. There was nobody around to reinforce the culture. I would have been the laughingstock of my high school class if it was known that I played Cajun music when I was twelve years old. They'd have tarred and feathered me.

"When I was a kid, the black people were just called Cajuns. Some would call themselves Creoles just like some of the white people would call themselves Creoles. Nobody really knew what a Creole was. Anything that was of hardy stock could be a Creole. But then somebody came down here and said the blacks are Creole and the whites are Cajun. The musicologists and the anthropologists have pretty well categorized who's who.

"A good while back I would go to the black people's dance and I got, 'Hey, Mark, come on in. Let me buy you a beer my man.' And after a while I was drinking with my friends and I said, 'You know, I really feel shitty. I come to your place—you buy me this beer, you welcome me and I feel great to be here. You're nice people, wonderful people making me feel welcome. But the thing about that is if you come to my scene, come into my dance, five minutes later people are going to be picking a fight with you because you're black.' And that's how it is. You as a white person can go in the black scene. But let not the black person come in the white scene. It's like kicking a hornet's nest. That feeling is still very prevalent and alive down here. It's too bad, too bad."

6

BY THE 1940s, thanks to the movies and the imaginary world of opulence they created, California, the land of perpetual summer, had become an American El Dorado. In New York or Chicago, men with names like Rockefeller or McCormick still ruled the landscape from high, urban towers. Wealth and social position were hereditary. California was different. Working-class men with a winning smile could become national heroes overnight; drugstore cowgirls in tight sweaters could parlay an abundant bosom into membership in the film pantheon. A million dollars could be earned with a wink, a smile could yield a palace. And it never got cold.

California meant abandonment. There were no roots, no ties, no excess baggage of tradition. Herbalists, witches, nudists, scientologists, taoists, phrenologists, alchemists, and Methodists migrated west to bask beneath the palm trees.

But a sign on the gates to Nirvana said WHITE ONLY. Of course, there were a few exceptions. Hi-Hat Hattie McDaniel, the recipient of the White Women's Christian Temperance Association's dramatic arts medal, won an Academy Award for best supporting actress in 1939. She was Mammy in *Gone With the Wind*. At the awards dinner, she had to sit in the back of the room at a table away from the white performers and technicians. In her acceptance speech, MGM forced her to say she was a credit to her race. Stepin Fetchit was a Hollywood staple in the 1940s. He was an actor with more than twenty years' film experience, but was only allowed to play ignorant, shuffling servants. He did it so well his name became a common noun of derision.

So it was not Hollywood and its dreams of the good life in the sunshine that brought blacks to the West. Rather, it was the same lure that took them from Mississippi to Chicago—jobs and bigger paychecks. In 1930 there were only eighty thousand blacks in California. During World War II, the plentiful jobs at defense plants changed that. When the bomb factories opened and assembly-line jobs became available, blacks in Texas, Arkansas, and Louisiana boarded the Santa Fe and headed to California. By 1950 there were 462,000 blacks in the state and more were coming every day. When they came, they brought the blues with them. The agreeable, sunny life on the West Coast imparted to the music a more mellow, sophisticated flavor.

I boarded the latter-day equivalent of the old Santa Fe, a nonstop jet to Los Angeles. When the plane landed, I gave Eddie "Cleanhead" Vinson a call. His wife, Bernice, answered the phone. "Sure," she said, "come on over." The Vinsons lived in Watts, the Harlem of Los Angeles, about thirty miles, three freeways, and four income brackets away from the San Fernando Valley where I was staying.

As I drove down the San Diego Freeway, cut across to the Santa Monica, and inched left on the Harbor Freeway, I thought about Cleanhead and the first time I met him. Eddie Vinson was born in Texas and worked his way to New York touring with Big Bill Broonzy in the Lil Green show in the 1940s. In New York he joined the Cootie

Williams Orchestra playing alto sax. Then, in 1945, he formed his own band and played the Club Zanzibar in New York. Charlie Parker learned the blues playing with Cleanhead. So did John Coltrane. In the mid-1950s Cleanhead and Bernice moved back to Houston, their hometown. Cleanhead taught music for a while, but he developed asthma and the climate wasn't right for him. So he moved to California.

Cleanhead played with everybody from Count Basie to Cannonball Adderley to Jay McShann. List the blues and jazz clubs all over America and Europe and Eddie Vinson's been there, singing the Cleanhead Blues:

> *Folks call me Mister Cleanhead,*
> *Just because my head is bald.*
> *But with the stuff that I use*
> *I don't need no hair at all.*

I met Cleanhead in the early 1970s at a blues revival show at the old Municipal Auditorium in Atlanta. He was a headliner, along with Big Mama Willie Mae Thornton, T-Bone Walker, Pee Wee Crayton, and Big Joe Turner. When I got there, everybody was sitting around in chrome-and-leatherette chairs in a dingy dressing room.

"Hey, boy," T-Bone said when I came in, "where can I get some whiskey?"

"You can't today," I said. "This is Sunday. All the liquor stores in Atlanta are closed on Sunday."

"Bullshit," T-Bone growled, "bullshit. This is Atlanta ain't it? Auburn Avenue's out there ain't it? Bullshit. I'll get some whiskey." And he got up and left. Auburn Avenue is the black main street of Atlanta. Most blues musicians from Bessie Smith on have played there, usually at

the Royal Peacock Club. T-Bone was back in ten minutes
with a fifth of bourbon.

"I told you I'd get some whiskey," he said. "Ain't no
way I'm not gonna get whiskey on Auburn Avenue."

He started passing the booze around. The show
started late and we were all deep into the bottle when Big
Mama Thornton opened with "Ball and Chain," a song
she wrote and Janis Joplin made famous. Big Mama finished and Big Joe was next. But he was held prisoner by
the chrome arms of his chair. He stood up and walked
across the floor giggling. The chair stayed around his massive hips like some Bauhaus bustle, wiggling and shaking
with every step until it fell off at the dressing room door.
He laughed. We drank. We drank so much that T-Bone
was unable to play. He stood onstage in front of a curtain
making pantomime licks on his guitar, while behind the
curtain Pee Wee Crayton plugged his instrument into the
sound system and imitated him. The audience never knew.

In the dressing room, Cleanhead and I were left alone
with the bottle. I stood up for a minute and Cleanhead
slammed a right hook into my stomach.

"Lose some weight, motherfucker," he said.

"But Cleanhead," I gasped, "I'm not that fat. Look at
Joe Turner."

"Ha! That mean old fat ugly Joe Turner? I hate him.
Lose some weight."

Now, fifteen years later and no thinner, I was pulling
off the Harbor Freeway and driving up Vernon Avenue
to see Cleanhead again. I hoped his idea of physical ther-
apy had changed.

As I knocked on the door of the white two-story house,
nestled between a church and some older apartments, I
realized that poverty in California is so different from the

American stereotype, it often appears that even the poor are rich. The weather is always warm and, instead of tenements, there are neat one- and two-story houses. They're often unpainted, but the oppression never seems as great as it does in the Delta shacks or the five-floor walkups on Chicago's South Side. The Vinsons lived in the biggest house on the block, but they took the caution of dead-bolt locks.

"Come on in," Bernice said, "Ed's not here right now. He's down the street. I'll call him home." She picked up the phone, called a neighborhood tavern and asked for Ed Vinson.

"Ed," she said, "that man's here who's doin' the book. Yeah. Come on home."

Both the living room and dining room were large, but they were shrouded in shadows. Across the dining room wall were a collection of golf trophies Vinson had won. Bernice continued to watch a soap opera until Cleanhead showed up. He was wearing a blue barret and the beard and mustache he'd worn for so many years was shaved to only a whisker of its former self.

Cleanhead sat down next to me on the white couch. He'd had a few drinks, and my stomach tightened instinctively. I reminded him we had met years before in Atlanta.

"Oh, yeah man," he said as he reached out and held my hand, "and 'Bone was there. He lost his guitar. He come back and didn't know where his guitar was. I had a lot of fun that night. You know what I done? I went and told T-Bone, I say, 'T-Bone, Joe say you ain't singing shit. And that's what caused the argument that night. That's what caused it. And I was just laughin'. That was fun. But you know what? We left T-Bone in Atlanta. He didn't make the plane that night. Me and Joe came back together."

His voice is low and his thoughts wander as he sits there squeezing my hand. T-Bone is dead, so is Big Mama Thornton, Pee Wee Crayton, and Big Joe Turner.

"Recently, I brought Joe's proclamation back from Kansas City for the funeral—when they were buryin' him. The mayor of Kansas City signed it and everything and I brought it back when they were burying him. Big Joe— we was good friends."

He stopped for a minute, lit a Camel, and began talking about his career, about how Eddie Vinson became Cleanhead.

"It was back in, oh, 1939 and, you know, we were puttin' stuff on our hair to make it shine. You know, to make it look like white folks' hair. And so, I was usin' something with lye and shit in it. And it started takin' my hair out. So I started wearing a stocking cap, like a lady's stocking, over my head. One day I took it off and all the hair come off with it. So, consequently, I shaved it off. And I got more broads! Everybody wanted to feel it. Everybody thought it was sexy.

"I'm the first. Yul Brynner and all them were after me. They came way behind—but you know all that shit. At the Apollo Theater, you know, back there with Cootie Williams, he called me Cleanhead. And the way things happened, we were playing "Things Ain't What They Used to Be" and we started playing, *a-blee-ba-da-wah*, like that— and Cootie says, 'Sing something,' and I sang, 'I love my baby but my baby don't love me. She said good-bye Mister Cleanhead . . .' And I guess that stuck.

"Some people say I play like Charlie Parker. But, man, there's so much difference between me and Charlie, you know what I mean? Then on the Mercury label, years ago, I made a workup on 'Kidney Stew.' You know that song, boy? Yeah, well I'm going way back on you, boy. This is history I'm tellin' you. I never was a man who liked glory. But in the years from the big band to the seven-piece band through the quartet, I acquired Ray Garland, Johnny Coltrane, lots of little kids. Cannonball and those boys. But you don't never hear anybody say nothing. Don't never hear anybody talk about these things. But I'm not afraid to say it because it's all fact. It's all documented. But nobody's ever put it, you know, down like it's supposed to be.

"In that New York era I was a trailblazer. They used to call me the trailblazer. They'd send me down in the territories to feel 'em out. They'd send me and Louis Jordan and then they'd send others."

Vinson puffs again on his cigarette and leans closer to me. His mind is reeling backward. He's left New York now and is back in Texas.

"Papa used to play in the speakeasies. Grandpaw used to play the do-si-do and all that other stuff on the fiddle for the white folks. He was the only black man to have a band down there in Texas who could play the do-si-do. Square dance, you know. I've seen fellas that used to come down the street with a guitar. You didn't have paved streets. It was sandy streets and here come a man playing a guitar for a glass of water or a dime—he'd sit on your front porch and play all day.

"But I was lucky enough to come from a middle-class family. You know, Papa worked at the packing house, the one that supplied the whole navy with meat. On a rainy day and the man can't see what they're bringing out of the packing house—we'd eat good. All of 'em did it during them days, black and white.

"See, back in Texas, when you came to high school, you either played football or basketball or got you a horn.

That was your thing to do down in Texas. It was more of a free state than in Mississippi and Georgia and Alabama. You understand what I mean? These are important things I'm telling you, little boy. I want you to absorb them. Don't let it go away. So I played football. And I got kicked. They got me in the neck and I said no, no, no. And I went and got me a horn. Right then. I went right to the man and say, 'Do you have a horn?' And my daddy bought me a horn.

"See, when I first met Bird he was playing the blues thing with Jay McShann. I met him in Shreveport. At the time I made these songs, "Person to Person," "Cherry Red"—that was what's happening at this particular time, you understand? You know Muddy Waters? Muddy, God bless him, he taught more kids about the blues. Now, I knew the Wolf. But my favorite man is Big Bill Broonzy. Lookie here. Lookie here, boy. He liked me. He liked me—Eddie Vinson. He liked Eddie Vinson. In the years when I was a star and he was still in Chicago, he'd come to my room with a brand-new box. And he'd say, 'How's it sound? How's it sound?' And I'd be tired. And I'd been smoking and was a high motherfucker, yeah, all that shit. Big Bill. That's my man. I liked LeRoy Carr and I liked all them, but Big Bill was something to me.

"I never had no problems no way. All during the years, I never had no problems. I never wanted to be big enough to have problems. I just wanted to be just like where I can have this here. You know?—my house and my garden. I been out digging in my garden today, turning the ground so we can have our little garden. It's nice. Sometimes you get tomatoes, green beans, strawberries. Sometimes you get so much you don't have space for it and you have to give it away.

"I just like to stay here and enjoy myself. Play a few gigs, make my wife happy and my little grandchildren— and that's about it. But Norman Grantz called and he wants me to make another album. Which I want to do because I'd like to sling a little shit—you know, about the way things are today. I gotta get a little political, make people understand the world the way it is. Not that I'm hungry or anything like that. But I'm gonna try to slip some politics in there.

"But, little boy, that's all I'm gonna tell you," Vinson said, and he let go of my hand and slumped back on the couch.

I turned off the tape recorder and stood up.

Bernice came back in the room. I smiled and left.

After I got back home, I waited for Jack and Betty Miller to come pick me up. The Millers migrated to Los Angeles from Chicago where Jack was a printer. He printed *Playboy* magazine by day and haunted blues joints at night. He moved to California in search of a better life printing catalogues. The job was good for a while, but things turned sour and he was soon out of work. The sunlight and palm trees were seductive, but soon the Millers became homesick for the blues. Only in L.A., they couldn't find it. That's when they got involved in a fledgling organization called the Southern California Blues Society.

The Millers were driving a battered old Chevrolet of indeterminate color. It was a perfect car to use for a nighttime trip into the bowels of Watts. By day, the California sunshine could hide the tragic poverty of Watts, the scene in 1965 of one of the largest race riots in the nation's history. But at night the dark shadows and wide, deserted streets gave the area and ominous feeling. We passed boarded-up store fronts and looked at the vacant expressions on the faces of the few people who were outside.

When the Watts riots began, white America was shocked. Wasn't California paradise? How could people who lived there become angry enough to burn and loot? Weren't the palm trees enough?

After the riots ended, after the last smoldering fire was snuffed out, a governmental commission from Washington decided to find out what caused enough frustration and despair at the edge of Nirvana to make people defy the law. The bureaucrats from Washington interviewed a lot of people, spent day after day traveling the charred streets, and came up with the same conclusion Southern whites had used to justify the civil rights protest movement: The riffraff did it.

The commission decided it was outside agitators of sorts, recent migrants to the area, unschooled in the ways of urban life, who smashed the plate-glass windows and burned the buildings. For people who didn't know the ghetto, it was a satisfying theory. The "good Negroes" would never have done that. The "good Negroes" were happy and knew their place. It was the riffraff who caused the Watts riots, just as it was the outside agitators who started the civil rights movement in Alabama and Mississippi.

The truth was different. Later surveys showed that many of the rioters were employed, long-time residents of Watts. They were not rooted in the rural life of the South but were streetwise in the ways of the city. Oddly enough, it was the church and its promise of a sweet by-and-by that had kept the South from being besieged by rioting, just as it was the church that gave the civil rights movement the moral underpinnings that made it successful.

But the church had lost its hold in Watts. California was supposed to be the ultimate American heaven; the by-and-by had come to pass. And it was almost as segregated as Sunflower County, Mississippi. God receded and the riots began.

The Millers and I talked about the blues as we crossed the streets of Watts on the way to Smoky's Pioneer Club.

"When we first moved out here, we got homesick for the blues," Betty said, raising her voice above the blaring sound of an oldies rock and roll station coming from the dashboard speaker. "We'd go into the black neighborhoods and they'd just be little bars and stuff. But we couldn't find any good music. Then one night we went to the Parisian Room and heard Margie Evans and Joe Tex. It was Joe Tex that attracted us. Anyway, afterward we went up to Margie and asked her if there was anywhere we could go to hear the blues. Well, we exchanged telephone numbers and a couple of weeks later she called and said some radio people were going to start a blues society. So, here we are, three and a half years later. I've been president of the society, and now Jack is."

"Listen," Jack said, "there's Big Joe." The familiar beat of Turner's "Shake, Rattle and Roll" reverberated through the car.

"Oh, we were very close," Betty said. "I was with him when he died. There've been so many who have died out here. You know, we lost Pee Wee Crayton—in the last two years we lost Pee Wee, Big Mama Thornton, Curtis Mayfield. You know, of course, that Pee Wee and Eddie Vinson have known each other for twenty-five or thirty years. I think it's been very hard on Ed psychologically. With Joe Turner and all. I think it's been very hard. And then Big Mama Thornton passed, and her sister is the only one left in that family. Big Mama didn't leave much money to bury her and so the Blues Society, we had a big benefit and it was really nice—the letters and checks that came from all over the country. They were just beautiful letters and sometimes they'd send a dollar or two. We got letters from everywhere, from all over. Like from Indiana. And it makes you stop and think: Who knows Big Mama Thornton in Indiana?"

"Shake, Rattle and Roll" was over and the disc jockey was screaming, but I was remembering another Joe Turner lyric:

> *You so beautiful,*
> *But you gotta die someday.*
> *All I want's a little lovin'*
> *Before you pass away.*

"I'm just coming to the realization that it's a real clique thing out here," Betty said. "The blues. I mean, when we first started meeting we had a few people come. But it's still the same people. It's a regular little clique."

"You know what's happened in California?," Jack said. "The young whites have really caught on to the blues. The majority of our shows we do in a white area. We have all-black entertainment and the majority or our audience, ninety-five per cent, is white."

We pulled up at the corner of Eighty-eighth Street and Vermont, got out and locked the car. A sign above the corner door said, SMOKY'S PIONEER CLUB. Inside, an audience of middle-aged black people were sitting at the bar and at small tables in front of a bandstand. A white woman in a crew cut, wearing jeans and a T-shirt with a pack of cigarettes protruding from rolled-up sleeves, was hunched over a pool table.

We sat down and ordered a quart of beer. Jack and Betty were regulars here and they waved to friends as we waited for the waitress. As in most blues clubs, once you're off the ghetto streets, fear vanishes. Away from its urban landscape, Smoky's could be a neighborhood bar in any city on any Friday night.

Smoky Wilson was outside talking to some friends. Jack and I decided to join him. We stood under a streetlight while Smoky explained that he bought the club with money from a trucking accident. He had been a Chicago truck driver. One day he smashed his rig, was hospitalized, and lost a leg. His insurance money paid for his move west and there was enough money left to open the Pioneer Club. He played hard-edged Chicago blues that had not been mellowed by the low-keyed influence of Los Angeles.

"Hey, man," a short man in a soiled golf cap said, interrupting my conversation with Smoky, "ain't you the one writin' the book about the blues?"

I said I was.

"Well, man, then I'm the dude you need to talk to. I used to be with Elmore James. Oh, yeah, man, me and Elmore, we traveled all around, you know, back in the fifties."

"Then you were a Broom Duster," I said, remembering that James had been billed as Elmore James and the Broom Dusters.

"Say what?"

"A Broom Duster."

"Naw, man, I played in the band. Hey. You from Mississippi?"

"Georgia," I answered.

"Nice country," the Broom Duster said. "I'm goin' back to Mississippi soon. Gonna bring some people out here to work. 'Cept they won't. Black peoples won't work, you know that? Now these Mexicans, you can count on them to work. I got Mexicans working for me now. And, man, they'll work all the time."

I listened a little longer to the virtues of migrant labor and went back inside the club. The band was playing and the Broom Duster had itchy feet. He began a long dance routine that involved most of the women in the club. He would jitterbug with one, dance into the corner and reappear with another doing an exaggerated tango. Each time he passed our table he would look at me, point and laugh. Woman after woman appeared in his arms, some fat, others thin, some towering above him, others standing on tiptoes.

We listened to the band for an hour or more as we knocked back a couple of quarts of beer and watched the Broom Duster's choreography. Smoky Wilson's music was appropriate for his middle-aged audience, particularly if they were migrants from Chicago. Get a cold wind to whistle through the door and they'd feel right at home.

"That's Smoky's girlfriend," Betty said, pointing to a woman at one of the front tables who had just finished a round with the Broom Duster. "And that," she nodded at the woman sitting alone behind the bar, "is his wife."

I wondered if they knew each other, but decided not to ask. The set ended and we got up to leave. The Broom Duster came over and pointed at me one last time. Smoky was a gracious host and as he thanked us for coming, he glanced at his wife who stood, unsmiling, giving him a piercing evil eye. We left and walked toward the car. In the shadows near an alley, a man was arguing with a woman. The words were harsh and as we got into the car he pushed her back against the brick wall. She squealed and I saw the glint of a switchblade knife. We locked the doors and drove off.

From Watts we inched across the maze of freeways to Hollywood, a ghetto of another sort. On celluloid, Hollywood has glamor and glitter. But driving down Hollywood Boulevard past the old Chinese Theater, which has lost its status as a palace and become just another suburban twin movie hall, we swerved to avoid what looked like the cast of *New Wave Hookers* milling in front of the Pussycat Theater. Even the tinsel has become tarnished. Hollywood, like everything else in America, has moved to even more distant suburbs, leaving behind the shell of fading glamor.

We pulled into a parking lot across from the old Hollywood Roosevelt Hotel. There had once been live musical broadcasts from this landmark, but now it was on its last legs, trying to spruce up for another adolescence with cosmetics. The smell of freshly applied pink and purple paint filled the lobby as we walked through in search of a group of white boys who had been hired for the night to play the blues.

We found them in an old ballroom. The crowd wasn't big and the waitresses seemed more interested in quitting time than hustling drinks. On the stage the band sounded more like The Rolling Stones than anything you'd hear at Smoky's Pioneer Club. Some of the musicians had just finished work in *Crossroads*, a movie about the blues. I'd seen the film, but because it rang so false, I kept my knowledge to myself.

When the set ended, a few musicians came over to speak to Betty. The band was packing up and the waitresses were clearing stale drinks and empty glasses off tables. We left. During the ride home there was only the sound of the radio, playing old rock and roll.

The next morning I drove to Pasadena to see Johnny Otis. Purists wouldn't call Otis a blues man. But I would. He traveled across the country in the 1950s and 1960s with the Johnny Otis show, probably the best rhythm-and-blues package ever assembled. He also had a big R&B hit, "Willie and the Handjive."

Until a few years ago, Otis lived in Watts, performing at the Barrelhouse Club and raising chickens in his backyard. But now he has retreated to the suburbs. I pulled up in front of his house, a long, sprawling rancher with a wire fence around it. A bus with THE JOHNNY OTIS SHOW emblazoned on its side was in the front yard. On the fence a red-and-white sign said BEWARE OF THE DOG.

There was no one around so I walked cautiously toward the gate. I didn't want my luck to change in a confrontation with a pit bull or a Doberman.

"Hello," I shouted at the gate. No answer. And no dog. I waited a minute or two. Maybe I should go to a phone booth and call so he could put the dog away. But I didn't. Instead, I inched the gate open a foot or two and shouted again. "Hello." Still no one answered. I was about to leave when one of Otis's sons came out the front door. "C'mon in," he said, "Dad's expecting you." Still no sign of the dog.

The walls in the living room were covered with paintings Otis had done of the blues—pictures of smoky bars and a striking portrait of Little Esther Phillips, his greatest discovery. There were also sculptures and masks that looked like updated African totems. Against one wall was a vibraphone. Like the bus out front, it was labeled THE JOHNNY OTIS SHOW.

After a few minutes, Otis walked in. He's over sixty-five, obviously older than his publicity pictures. His beard is gray and there are signs of arthritis in his hands. But when he speaks, his voice is familiar. It's a little huskier than it sounded on "Handjive," but the same cadence and rhythms are there. Yet there's always a shock when you meet Otis because he's white. His wife is black and he adopted black culture as his own when he was a child in Vallejo, near San Francisco. On the radio or on records, he sounds black because, in spirit, he is.

We talked for a while about West Coast blues men, about T-Bone Walker and Roy Milton and Charlie Brown, about Nat "King" Cole and the early days of rhythm and blues. Then he began to explain the attraction Los Angeles had for the musicians who migrated here.

"It was supposed to be the land of opportunity and all that crap," he said. "We did have an advantage in the weather and I guess that figured strongly. Los Angeles really had the same attraction it held for all other black enterainers and musicians—all other people, for that matter.

"If you're from a place like Louisiana where it's terribly wet and damp in the summer and cold as hell in the winter, California has an attraction. But what was happening here during the war was the new war machine, the aircraft industry. All the defense plants were here. And it drew a lot of people from Texas, Oklahoma, and Louisiana."

But even before there were defense jobs, the blues had migrated to California.

"I'm from Berkeley," Otis said, "and the music is just part of the black community. The blues particularly. It was in the air. I didn't think of being a musician until I saw Count Basie's band at the World's Fair in San Francisco in 1939. And then all of a sudden, I was on fire. I'd never seen anything like that. I remember Joe Jones, the great drummer. After I saw him I wanted to be a drummer. But the first man to get me started trying to play anything was a man named Otis Matthews. Count Otis Matthews, we called him. He was a boogie-woogie barrelhouse piano player down from the Mississippi Delta somewhere.

"But I tell you what I heard as a kid that influenced me. I didn't know the name of it and I didn't know who the artist was at the time, but it turned out to be "Terraplane Blues" by Robert Johnson. There was a guy who lived across the street from us who was a railroad porter and he would go to Chicago and back to Oakland and he would bring those old seventy-eights of Robert Johnson. It wasn't until years later when I heard those records again that I found out he was a legendary man. So those kind of country blues and Count Basie's band were really my influences. And right near my home were two, we call 'em holiness churches. And we would go there to get the free graham crackers and chocolate milk. Also, all the pretty little girls were there. So I was exposed to gospel music, too.

"Anyway, Count Matthews put a band together and he made me his drummer. And he told me the beats to play. He called it 'shave-and-a-haircut-six-bits.' Nowadays everybody knows that as the Bo Diddley beat—and of course, it's the handjive beat. Before that it was the hambone beat and before that the West African beat.

"Well, anyway, we went to Reno, Nevada, to get this job that was supposed to pay forty-five dollars a week apiece. At that time, my father was making about twenty-six dollars a week. So, forty-five dollars a week—man! But when we got there we found out it was forty-five dollars for the three of us—fifteen dollars each. And we had to pay room and board. At the end of every week we ended up owing the man who owned the hotel. So when George Morrison's band came though town and they needed a drummer, I joined up. I went from Reno to Omaha and from Omaha to here. I'm a native Californian but I got to Los Angeles roundabout."

As Otis talked about his early days in music, I began to realize how tough it was to make the decision to be a black with white skin. I asked him about it.

"You have to be old enough to understand how perilous that was. You took your life in your hands. Many times we had terrible experiences. Jesus Christ, it's a wonder I'm still alive. You see, my father was the grocer in the black community in Oakland. I don't remember anything but black people. I was raised there. Black kids would come by and we played out in empty lots together. There's nothing unique about that. But then you get to the teenage years. That's when social pressures will pull you apart, because now the girls are going to be young ladies and the boys are going to be young men. And it was a no-no to have blacks and whites together. But I just refused to go anywhere else. That was where I wanted to be and I wasn't gonna leave it. And I didn't.

"For me the black culture was a superior culture. It was a culture I appreciated and one I was happy in. And it's very creative. It's a wonderful place to be. I wouldn't leave it to go to heaven. Then or now."

Otis came to Los Angeles and became leader of the sixteen-piece house band at the Club Alabam'. He had a hit recording of "Harlem Nocturne" and went on the road with the Ink Spots. But despite the postwar boom, he had to change the band after the tour.

"I cut my band down to just a couple of horns and changed the character of it because I had noticed through the years that what people really responded to were boogie-woogies on the piano and twanging guitars, electric guitars, and a drummer who could play a good strong beat. And that's what we opened with in Watts at the Barrelhouse in 1948.

"But I had this idea. I went to my partner and I said, 'Remember the old minstrel shows down South, remember their stage presentations?' Now, when I say minstrel shows—I'm not talking about the white shows. What I'm talking about is the *Silas Green from New Orleans Show*, the *Rabbit Foot Minstrels*. So I said, 'Why don't we put together something and advertise it almost like a carnival coming to town?' Well, he wanted to know what acts I'd get. And I said, 'Get nobody! We got all the acts! Right here in the Barrelhouse! Our own people!' We had Kathy Cooper, known as the Queen of the Blues, and we had Pete Lewis, the great guitarist sensation. So we did it. We went to San Diego. We took placards down there and I used that old yellow, orange, and black combination. It looked like the old carnival and circus posters. We had a tremendous crowd that night.

"Well, in the Barrelhouse, I was cutting some records with Little Esther Phillips and we had some hits in fifty and fifty-one. So we went on the road and I used the same format, only I called it the *Rhythm and Blues Caravan*. When we got back to town in fifty-three or fifty-four, I got a disc jockey show. And I put on another show in San Diego. I rented what used to be the ice rink. That night we had something like eight thousand people. I'd never seen anything like it! Oh, maybe I saw something like it when we were on the road in Kansas City or Atlanta, but this was just a little jive-ass local thing. And I couldn't believe it.

"But what was more amazing was the racial makeup of that audience. It really threw me for a loop. It was mostly white. My radio manager went along with me for a lark and when he saw that audience he said, 'Oh shit, man, something's happening.'

"So when we got back to town we went over to Channel Eleven, the TV station. And the manager said he'd give us a show at seven-thirty on Thursday night. He said, 'How you like that?' And I said, 'Shit, man, prime time! I like that fine.' And he said, 'Well, you won't like it because it's opposite the *Sixty-four Thousand Dollar Question*,' which was the biggest TV show at the time. But I said we'd take it. He told me we wouldn't have any audience, but he didn't know what was happening. Hell, I didn't either. I just hoped somebody watched. But we got ratings. People began flocking to the station and it was just a little jive-ass show.

"Well, that was during the fifties. Then it was the sixties and The Beatles came along and *I* couldn't get arrested. But now it's gotten nice again. Now I'm beginning to see large numbers of young people listening to my music. But of course they're all white. The tragedy is that we don't have young black kids coming yet. But that may happen before it's over with. I hope so. Because this tradition is—well, let me put it this way. If you go to a fine Cantonese restaurant, you really don't want to peek in the kitchen and see a Swede cooking. You want some good Chinese food and you expect a Chinese chef," Otis said.

"I've been accused of racism because I need a black band. Well, that's the reason I need it. It's a cultural reason. Jewish cantors are hardly gonna be Irish. I mean, you can talk all this history and roots to these black kids but if they don't know who Mahalia Jackson is, if they've never heard of Langston Hughes or Count Basie, then they don't really know who they are.

"You know, in the last few years, we've developed a black American middle class. A black version of the yuppies. And for the most part, they're not interested in their blackness. Or their African heritage, or even their African-American heritage. So I guess we can discount them.

"But the other folks—they're so wrapped up in poverty and cocaine, so crowded in the ghetto. It's a sad, sad situation. The blues life is the Afro-American experience. Only now, it's a different kind of oppression. In the old days, as bad as it was, there were some sweet touches. We had our cultural integrity. We had our own neighborhoods, our nightclubs, our restaurants. We don't have that anymore. We don't have any of that anymore.

"You go to Watts, where I lived for so many years, and you take your life in your hands going out on the street. We had a nice place there. Two nice places. Now, you've got to be careful everywhere, and not just in the black community. But surely you've got to be careful in the black community because it's the most oppressed and the most depressed. I breathed a sigh of relief when we left Watts.

"Think of the disparity gap between white and black incomes and how it continues to broaden. And then, of

course, our good liberal establishment brought us the wel-
fare syndrome. I don't mean to suggest that conservatives
have the answer because they're heartless and that's even
worse.

"But, you know, we've never really done what's right
by our people, and I mean all people. When somebody's
poor in a country with as much as this country has, the
country's supposed to get right under him and lift him up.
Not for charitable reasons but because it's the right thing
to do. It's the smart thing to do. But we don't do that. It's
all for profit and all for power and all for our mighty
gods—the multinational corporations. And they've forgotten about people. You know, don't tell me about the
trickle-down theory. It may have a fancy name, but none
of that shit works.

"When you get rid of racism, then what are you gonna
do about predatory capitalism? They're both in the same
bolt of yarn. Some people ask me, 'Are you a Communist?'
I say, 'No, I'm trying to be a Christian. Do I have to be a
communist because I know predatory capitalism is evil and
doesn't meet the needs of our people?' You talk of profit.
Is that our god? No. I like the idea of free enterprise, man,
but show me some. I haven't seen any. I'm an old rug
merchant—I'd love some free enterprise."

Otis shifted in his chair and wiped his forehead.

"You sound like a preacher," I said.

"I've been pastor of the Landmark Church for seven
years," he answered, "and an ordained minister for about
eleven. I wasn't self-ordained. I didn't see any flash of light.
I belonged to one of the big Baptist churches in town. One
Sunday morning, I met Sam Cook outside the church.
We'd both been on the road. This is a church with about

two thousand people and we went in and the preacher—
he really didn't mean any harm—but he said, 'We're glad
Brother Sam and Brother Johnny are back with us this
morning and one day they're gonna leave the devil's music
alone and come on back home.' And Sam whispers to me,
'Did that motherfucker really say that?' I said 'Yeah,' and
that's the last time either of us ever went back to that
church.

"I was in the Baptist church all my life and, you know,
I got tired of hearing about the devil's music and the sinful
blues people. In the black community our churches are
carbon copies of the fundamentalist Southern white
churches. Somewhere in the past I guess some white
preacher came to the black preacher and told him, 'That
stuff your people are doing out there is sinful.' But instead
of asking the white preacher if the European symphonic
music his congregation listens to was sinful—he couldn't
do that, of course—he carried that message to the pulpit
and he tied everyone up in knots. And we're still tied up
in knots. I know people who are intellectually above that
shit but they still can't fight their way out of it. They still
think the blues is sinful. Beautiful Afro-American art and
it's sinful. That's a bunch of shit. The whole world thirsts
for Afro-American music and many of our leaders would
have our own people turn their backs on it, on their own
thing.

"After I left the Baptist church I started going to a
little church down in the ghetto where Mother Bernice
Smith was the pastor. She thought it would be nice for me
to be a street evangelist. I told her, 'I don't deal in none
of that hocus-pocus. I won't go tell them about how Jesus
walked on the water.' I told her Christianity was a very

simple thing to me. Jesus said you love one another. That's about it. Brotherhood, forgiveness, and love. She said, 'That's about it.'

"As time went by she decided maybe I should be an ordained minister. And I said, 'Can't you just see people now, talkin' about Reverend Hand Jive?' Guess who ordained me? Bishop Gatemouth Moore. A big, big star in his day. Wrote 'Did You Ever Love a Woman?' He stopped singing the blues to become a preacher."

I asked Otis about his reputation as the chicken man of Watts.

"C'mon out back. I'll show you," he said. We walked out into his backyard, toward an area separated from the rest of the yard by chicken wire.

"I've got all kinds of chicken and geese and pigeons and ducks back there. But they're all gifts. That's how I got into the turkey business. One of my church sisters came here for a get-together and she knew I used to be the chicken man in Watts in the old days. And she also heard people brought me gifts. So she brings me two little turkeys and during the night one of 'em dies. So I call the hatchery and they had some on hand. So I bought some more just to keep that one she brought company. That's how I ended up with turkeys. I tried to raise them but I stopped because they are such a bitch."

We walked into the bird pen filled with winged creatures. He kicked a rooster aside.

"Now you better stay away from him. Stay away from that one. He was raised a fighting cock and so he thinks he's always got to be mean." The rooster started advancing again and Otis kicked it aside. He cooed at the pigeons, spoke softly to the ducks, and coaxed a peacock to open its tail. I kept my eye on the fighting cock.

Reverend Hand Jive had to do his weekly jazz-and-blues radio show that night, so I left to give him time to prepare it. But I still wondered about that dog I was supposed to fear.

"What about your dog, the one that made you put up the sign?" I asked.

"Oh, him? I'll show you. Hey! Wolf!" he called. Suddenly, tearing around the house came a full-sized Chihuahua.

"That's your dog?" I said. "But what about the sign out front?"

"Oh, that. That was here when we moved in. Just never bothered to take it down. C'mere, Wolf."

The Chihuahua nuzzled his hand. I walked to my car and headed back to Los Angeles.

Johnny Otis became a musician and latter-day preacher by conversion, I thought as I headed down the freeway into Hollywood, but Margie Evans, whose apartment I was driving toward, inherited both talents. Her father was a preacher, her mother a piano player. I passed a decaying movie palace, its neon signs glowing with yellows, greens, and red. It had been converted to an automobile showroom. Movies used to be the heart of the California dream; now it was the automobile.

A few blocks away was a neat apartment complex built in the 1950s. I was late, and Margie Evans was poking her head out the door waiting for me. She had been a singer with the old Johnny Otis shows, but hadn't been heard from much since.

Margie Evans is rotund, a blues singer from the mold of Bessie Smith and Ma Rainey. She's wearing an African print caftan and a tuft of gray hair springs out from beneath a matching turban. She ushers me to a seat in the living room. Her husband waves from the dining area as he tries to watch the news on television. There's little small talk with Margie Evans. She has a mission. She's convinced that the National Academy of Recording Arts and Sciences shouldn't let white people win Grammys for blues.

Before I could catch my breath, she had launched into her subject, standing above me as I sat and listened. As she talked, her husband eased up the volume of the television. But a modulated announcer's tales of floods, pestilence, and arms negotiations were no match for Margie Evans at full volume.

"You know what they doin' to the blues?" she said, starting on a low note. "Everything's money. That's what the people think now. Everything is for money. But the blues. The blues is a culture of a people."

Johnny Otis had said much the same thing, but he spoke in modulated tones of reason. Margie Evans had the spirit of Louisiana behind her. You could hear her church training in Shreveport in every sentence. This was not a talk with an ordained minister; this was church with a congregation of one.

"We, the Negro people, my ancestors before me, the people that were sold into slavery—people who had been messed around with by whomever—we became a home-made race—fifty percent of something, fifty percent of something else. Hell, we don't even know who in the devil we are. I can't claim I'm African can I? No. So what can I claim? I'm not Caucasian. I'm homemade! Hey! I got fifty percent of both of y'all.

"I always tell people, 'Don't ever start in the middle of the road to come to the beginning of a people. We are a people! Every people on the face of the earth got their own culture.' But they rape and rob us like we don't have it. So blues is a culture. It's not a low-down dirty art form.

"That's the reason I attacked the Grammys. I sent a letter to Bruce Iglauer at Alligator Records. I said, 'Bruce! It's all right for you to make money off those idiots in Chicago, but do not come to Margery Evans trying to make me believe that you understand the pain of my people. I've never been to a wailing wall or to a rabbi and talked to him about letting me wail. That's not part of my culture.'

"But everybody thinks they can cry my cry. But you can't do it. Listen, this pain that I'm feeling is from way down inside."

In the dining room, the volume goes up on the newscast. Tales of political chicanery begin to compete with Margie's sermon. But she adjusts and once again her sermon overpowers everything. Her husband inches his chair closer to the television.

"They talk about traditional blues. Traditional means what? Transcended from ancestors to descendants without writing anything down." A tea kettle whistles in the background. She ignores it and raises her voice another decibel.

Margie is humming now, a deep, resonant sound that is the essence of black music. "My grandmother showed me how to do that. Now steal it! I tried to spend hours talking to my daughter. I told her that if you had tried to make yourself, you'd make yourself so all the world would like you. But they taught the black man to hate himself. You see what I'm sayin'? Hate your people, your own music. And the idiots are still doin' it! Come on. Let's face it. Now you get somebody like me—and I'm not puttin' nobody down—I'm dealing with the stark realities."

Someone unseen has turned off the tea kettle. Margie continues.

"Hey! Let's go back and deal with the facts. Even though my mama cooked for Miss Ann, OK?—raised Miss Ann's children—in fact, Miss Ann's children sucked from my mama's breasts! And then to call my mama a nigger, you must be a crazy person!"

The sermon is veering away now. But as a congregation of one, I think it might be best to let her have her own way. She is towering above me and sweat is beading on her forehead.

"Then I must ask you, what is a nigger? When I was in school, it meant anyone who was offensive. It didn't mean the Negro race. So there's a whole lot of lies being told somewhere. And this new generation is getting ready to kill us all 'cause they say we're just a no-good sack of dogs.

"So now we all come out of the woodwork everywhere. Trying to say a little bit of truth so we can last a little longer. Because, you see, our culture is no longer the Negroes or the black adjective. And, incidentally, I'd rather be a noun, my dear, because I know the white man didn't make me a Negro. He might have made me an adjective, but he didn't make me a Negro.

"But see—we got to know our own history. All the white folks write the books about the blues. All the music in America came from the blues. Europeans have their own. But my people don't want nobody taking their stuff—and messing it up and putting their own little lousy words to it and their own meaning.

"Who is Margie Evans?" she shouted, reading my mind. "I'm a child of the King. I don't give a spit what they talkin' about—aw, just a blues singer. I know the Lord and he will make a way for me. Now you gonna say the blues is dirty music, see. You see the drunks and the sluts out there swinging their hips. That's the blues, you say. But I say no! It's a culture.

"But you know, if this world was mine and I was in control, I could get some money. But I can't get a loan. I can't keep a record company going. I'm in trouble up to my neck. I got to hustle gigs. Man calls me from Canada. He says, 'Are you available?' Yes! Man calls me from Boston. 'Can you be here?' Yes! And they say, 'Listen, can you pick up some gigs along the way?' and I say, 'Now let me tell you something about Margie Evans. I ain't no Mama Thornton! I ain't gonna hustle no highway trying to go to no dumps and dives and fight for them two little pennies. I don't want to be no hard-nosed, drunk, evil, mean black woman. So, son, do not characterize me like y'all did Mama Thornton. If I leave this world, I won't leave here bitter, saying, "I worked for all these peoples and they stole all my songs and I ain't got a dime." ' That ain't Margie Evans!"

A beautiful child walks in slowly, her eyes wide with apprehension. She whispers something to Margie, who stops in mid-sermon and tells the girl to go back and finish her meal.

"Poor little girl," she says. "Her mama's dead and she don't know her daddy." But seeing the child gives her new fuel. "We better tell the truth because all our children—be they white, be they black, be they Hispanic—are comin' up like idiots. Future generations are lost! That's why they giving in to dope! They have no hope for the future! I don't care how much education they have! You know, in the South we were all taught there is a God. But we got our children comin' up thinkin' God is money. They think it's in those Gucci's you wear. In your aerobics and your shower massages and all that bull. We got 'em thinkin' God

was sex until people got tired of all these teenagers havin'
babies. Babies, babies, babies! They're committing suicide
coming and going because they have no foundation!

"We got to give every man back what was his at birth.
And that is his culture! Don't you know that a man who
knows who he is and what he has contributed to the world
wouldn't have to run around here and steal and kill?"

Evans slowed to catch her breath and the sermon took
an autobiographical turn.

"I'm continuously amazed to listen to the elders in the
black community trying to explain what the blues is. Now,
I'm from a Christian family. It was always church, church,
church. My mother used to call the blues dirty music. So
most of what we heard in Shreveport, Louisiana, was country and western. My aunts and them used to go to the
Louisiana Hayride. When they heard the word blues they
thought about a bunch of dirty, low-down people hanging
out at the Highland Bar. So when I was a girl I didn't get
a chance to hear much blues until I went to Grambling
College. I'd hear that music and I'd say, 'That ain't low-
down and dirty! What are they talkin' about?'

"When I came to Los Angeles I worked as a ballad
singer at a bar called Tiki's in Monterey Park. Big Band.
I sang 'Misty,' 'The Nearness of You.' Then the man I was
workin' for asked me if I'd like to be the featured singer
with a man named Johnny Otis. I went to the Seventeen-
Seventeen Bar and Johnny Otis said, 'Can you sing the
blues?' I said, 'Naw. I don't sing no blues. I don't know
what you're talkin' 'bout.' Well, he started playin' those
twelve bars and I started singin'. And he said, 'Girl, you
ain't nothin but a blues singer.' And I said, 'I don't even
know what it is.'

"It amazes me continuously to hear older blacks talk

about the blues. They refuse to recognize the fact that they don't know what it is. They involve it with being poor. They involve it with being drunk. You know: 'My man done left me and my woman done gone and if that ship don't land they better not come back here and don't the moon look beautiful shinin' through the trees.'

"Now, the unique thing about the blues in Los Angeles—most of the people who came here from Louisiana and Texas, they didn't come from totally poor mentalities. Most of them were educated. They ain't dirty. You ain't gonna find no roaches crawling me. They're not snaggle-tooths and they know how to bathe their musty butts. These young people are so hip now. Look at Prince. Classy dressing. Not depressing. Out here we sing a music that's contemporary for the metropolitan area we live in. This is Los Angeles. I ain't sittin' down there in Leland, Mississippi, with Son Thomas.

"But let's face it. I would not have been able to make a dime if it had not been for young Caucasian students flocking in to see me. Let's face it. I been on shows by myself and with Johnny Otis and I ain't seen no blacks payin' to get in. What has happened with the music is that the Caucasians kept it alive."

I thanked Margie Evans for talking to me. She seems calmer now. "Y'all come back, you hear?" she says, and I drive off into the smog to look for a bar where Cleanhead Vinson is playing.

Cleanhead was playing at Musicworks, a dancehall in East L.A. When he plays the saxophone or sings, Cleanhead, despite the emotions his music generates, is impassive. He stands on stage, the band blasting behind him, and produces music that conjures up images of Kansas

City, of Texas Roadhouses with smoky overtones, of Saturday-night abandon. If anyone doubts there was blues before Muddy Waters, before the electric guitar, before rock groups co-opted it, Vinson is living proof. His is a good-time dance music guaranteed to make you forget your problems for at least twelve bars.

The next morning over coffee I decided to drive south to San Diego and talk to a husband-wife team, Jimmy and Jeannie Cheatham.

When most people think of the blues these days, they think of the early days of rock and roll, of music taken to Chicago by Mississippians on the great migration. But the music is more than that. The blues has become so much a part of rock, people forget it was first the backbone of jazz.

Before Muddy Waters, before Howlin' Wolf, before any bluesman picked up the first electric guitar, there was Big Joe Turner, Count Basie, Pete Johnson. And they were all in Kansas City. That city's musical tradition is mostly history now. Clubs like Piney Brown's, The Hole in the Wall, The Black and Tan, and the Hawaiian Gardens are all closed. Basie is dead and so is Big Joe. Only Jay McShann remains as a living testament to the blues and boogie-woogie sound that energized jazz in the early 1930s.

It's a two-hour drive to San Diego, but you never leave the city. The California dream of an air-conditioned hacienda and a palm tree on a quarter-acre lot has pushed its way through desert, sand dunes, and marshes. It's like a monster that squirmed its way from the Hollywood Hills, inched south to Orange County, and slithered down the coast. Its trail is interrupted only by a Marine base. Subdivisions and cars define California. The blues are here, but they wear a Hawaiian shirt and carry an overextended credit card.

I met the Cheathams in the bar at the Bahia Resort Hotel, a rambling building that was probably the height of luxury a decade or so ago. But as styles changed in Southern California, which they do daily, the Bahia seems less posh. In another ten years it will be quaint. Now it's only out-of-date. The Cheathams were sipping brandy and watching the last race from Santa Anita. Jimmy's hair has grayed and he looks a little like Count Basie. Jeannie is slim and sultry. Her eyes flash and there is an animation to her that can't be captured in photographs. Her beauty comes with movement—a nod, a wink, a smile.

Jimmy plays trombone and is a professor at the University of California at San Diego. As he talks, overtones of academia creep into his conversation. Jeannie, who's accompanied Big Mama Thornton, Big Joe Turner, Big Maybell, Jimmy Rushing, and Wynonne Harris and now sings in a growling, sometimes throaty voice as she plays the piano, acts as a chorus in our conversation. Like her singing, she is sophisticated and earthy.

"I was born in Birmingham, Alabama," Jimmy says, glancing occasionally at the television above the bar, "but I was raised in Buffalo. Then in World War Two, I was back in Alabama, in Anniston at Fort McClellen. After the war, I worked professionally in New York City, mostly with Chico Hamilton. I taught part-time at Bennington, about two days a week. Then I'd go into the recording studio and perform."

"I was born in Akron," Jeannie says, "Akron, Ohio. I went on the road with a band after Akron and spent most of my career in Canada. Then I met Jimmy in Buffalo and we started our sojourn."

"Before I started teaching at the University of California at San Diego, I taught at the University of Wisconsin in Madison," Jimmy says.

I ordered a bourbon and we began talking about the blues.

"The blues is very personal, it's like jazz, it's a way of life," Jimmy says. "The whole socioeconomic and political spectrum are involved. And the personal and emotional involvement all are a part of that way of life. You know, it's all involved in the migration. Everything is migratory. The use of the saxophone in blues, that's a result of coming out of the fields and into the city—out of the rice fields and cotton fields and coming to town. Off the docks and into the city. This is where the whole thing starts happening—a coming together, trading experiences—a way of life. The nature of the city, the nature of the environment dictates the total way of life. The city becomes a part of the music. It's not as if the days in the fields were wiped out. They aren't."

"Yeah," says Jeannie, "'cause when they had house-rent parties they still played boogie-woogie. Even in New York."

"Now, the house-rent party was the name of the game for gettin' down," Jimmy says, "and, you know houses of ill repute existed everywhere, too. Not just in New Orleans. And the blues was there. The blues is a way of life in terms of the life and personal experiences of an individual. The way it comes out in the music is from personal experience."

"And you know, when people sing the blues, they always sing about either love or money," Jeannie says.

"Yeah," adds Jimmy, "people are still interested in the blues because people are still poor, poor in spirit."

"Un hunh," says Jeannie.

"Economically," says Jimmy, beginning to warm to his subject and taking on the cadence of a preacher.

"Oh, yes," answers Jeannie.

"Socially, politically."

"That's right."

"And the expression of the blues is really one of the strongest ways of conveying that. Even with a great sense of humor."

"You know," says Jeannie, "we had some kids come down to see us when we were playing at the Sheraton over there. And they said, 'Oh, we really don't like the blues.' Their teacher made them come because they had to do a paper on it. 'We think that's old-time music,' they said. And I told them, 'You know anybody who's got a Ph.D?' They said yeah. I say, 'Is he driving a cab?' They say yeah. I say, 'Well, let me tell you, he's got the blues.' "

"But," I said, "it seems to me that fewer and fewer people are choosing the blues as their way of musical expression."

"There's a reason why," Jimmy says, "You see . . ."

"I'm gonna challenge that," says Jeannie, taking another sip of her brandy. "I think you're wrong, and I'm gonna tell you why I think you're wrong. Mainly, it's because every young white rock and roller reaps the benefit of the blues and they steal right and left. That's how The Rolling Stones—Mick Jagger will tell you in a minute where he got his songs. The Beatles, every one of the top rock-and-roll groups, all of them steal from the black blues. They put all this electronic stuff with it and then they call it their music. Most of them aren't honest enough to say where they got it."

"It took the British musicians to bring the blues back to America," Jimmy says.

"Right, you can believe that," Jeannie says.

"To accept what I call mass-consciousness in terms of communication . . . And they're making money with it . . ."

"Which beforehand the blues has always been in terms of race records . . ."

"I mean, they're really making money. The point is, they're making a living. They're making more than the originators."

"But the dichotomy of it is that most black kids aren't playing the blues, that's where you'll find the difference."

"Naw, they're not doing it."

"There's a similar association in terms of the Negro spiritual. These kids say that's slave times. But it's not slave times . . ."

"Yeah, but these kids, that's the way they feel."

"They've got to be aware that slavery is a mental state. So from the cotton fields we're into IBM now."

"Yeah. I know that's right. Where they get rid of you right before you retire."

"They got the blues."

"They got the blues, baby."

"You hear it every day. Big corporate people who thought they had it made."

"Had it made. You know, and they get cheated of their retirement," he snaps his fingers, "just like that."

"They had this man on TV the other night," says Jeannie, "who was fired after twenty-nine and a half years. Six months more would have made a difference in his family having a pension. That's the blues. The white-collar blues."

"Pain is like greed," Jimmy says. "It doesn't care who wishes to possess it. It's no respecter of persons. So I guarantee you, you gonna deal with greed, you gonna deal with pain. You want to know about the blues life now? Check out the families who are out in the streets, lying over street vents to keep warm. In Austin, in Detroit, it's the same thing as a Depression. That's why they've created the whole idea of a plantation concept in the first place. It went from the cotton fields to the factories, to high tech. They just got more people involved now, but we're mostly still on a plantation."

"Wait a few months, see what the oil people and the rich people everywhere will be like when they find out they ain't got no job," Jeannie says.

"It'll be the suburb as ghetto."

"What's that song?—'The Whole World Is a Ghetto.' Forget all this talk about good times. They said that in 1929 before the people jumped out of windows. You got roaches and cracks in the walls, it's a ghetto."

"Yeah," says Jimmy, "But each environment is entirely different. And it goes all the way back to Africa . . ."

"You're right, it's different," Jeannie says. "I had the chance to play with Big Joe Turner, T-Bone Walker, Big Maybell, Jimmy Rushing, Big Mama Thornton. All the different types of blues. And to accompany them was a unique experience. You become aware of how much alike they are and yet how different. You hang around with them two or three weeks and play every night with them and you get a chance to settle in and find out the common thread that goes through all of us. But, you know, back in Ohio, we never separated jazz and the blues."

"Like, if we played 'Misty,'" says Jimmy, "it'd be a ballad and yet the blues would be part of the expression."

"The lines between music get really blurry," Jeannie says. "There's all kind of blues. Twelve-bar blues, nine-bar, eighteen-bar. It's whatever a person has to say and how they want to say it."

"That's what makes it such a threat to people who don't truly accept freedom. They still want to . . ."

"Put it in a box."

"And to put something in a box is like putting a shackle on someone. And that's why the music itself—blues, jazz, even going back to the spiritual when the Fisk Jubilee Choir went to Europe—shook up everybody. It was freedom, and yet they sung a repertory of the European tradition."

"Most of the times the people who want to put everything in a different box are critics and people who write about the music and they're not musicians." She stopped and looked hard at me. "You might be one of 'em. You might be."

Later that night, I listened to the Cheathams for two sets. Jimmy led a seven-piece band behind Jeannie's piano and singing. There were no limits. Sometimes it was blues, with Jeannie's piano sounding more and more like Jay McShann, like boogie-woogie. Sometimes it was jazz transported from the swing era of Count Basie. But the Cheatham blues weren't lamenting the ghetto days of Chicago. They were talking to California today. As Jeannie sings: "It's just you and me, Baby, and the finance company."

The next morning I left San Diego, drove back through Los Angeles and on up Highway 5 to San Francisco. I wanted to travel through the heart of California, near the desert, because that's where America's new cotton kingdom lies. Alabama and Mississippi and Texas may brag about their cotton production, but California is where most of the bolls are picked. In Mississippi, the Delta is flat and black. The California cotton country is flat and sandy. God created the Delta; man made the San Joaquin valley. One side of the road—the side with sprinklers—is lush.

The other, where modern agriculture has not interfered, is barren.

It's a long ride, and to pass the time I listened to Mexican radio stations. Blacks were the workers in Mississippi cotton fields and the blues came from that experience. But in California, Mexican labor has become the field hands of choice. And so the blues from the land of cotton now has a Latin feel. This is the working-man's music of the latter twentieth century. And, just as New Orleans writers were ashamed of early jazz, forcing it to an underground of whorehouses and street corners, the Mexican music today is spurned by most people in the valley.

Closer to San Francisco, an announcer attempts a translation. The song just played, she said, is, "The midgets are angry because their mother has pinched them." Evidently, I am not the only one in the valley who doesn't understand Spanish.

There is an unrelieved sameness here. It lacks the character of the Delta, the allure of the bayous. It is agribusiness, not agriculture, and touring factories always makes me uncomfortable.

Finally, San Francisco. It costs a dollar to get into the city. You can leave for free. Even before Tony Bennett left his heart there, San Francisco had a reputation as the most European of American cities. It was also known for its toleration of whackos. Most of the fads in latter-twentieth-century America began on or near these hills where gold miners once walked. The beatniks started here and so did the hippies. The first topless dancers showed their stuff only a few blocks from the bookstores and coffeehouses where Allen Ginsberg read poetry. And when the country shifted to the greed of the pure-market economy, it was suburban Marin County that gave America the hot tub.

But greed had inched across the bay and into the city. North Beach, once the province of old Italian families and aging beats, was being gentrified. Houses or apartments were going for rates only stockbrokers could afford. I checked into a hotel that, five years before, had been a flophouse. Now it had been gentrified with daily high tea and flocked wallpaper. The old elevator still rattled and creaked as it ascended, but no one would consider it out-of-date anymore, only quaint. Once it had carried alcoholics, whores, and trembling street refugees away from reality. Now it transported the gotrocks and anglophiles to mid-afternoon cucumber sandwiches on the mezzanine.

Like New Orleans, San Francisco could have been a city filled with ghosts. But commerce sent the spirits flying. And with those spirits of hippies and long-forgotten beatniks went the blues.

For a while, after World War II, San Francisco had been a good blues town. Returning black soldiers were discharged there and there was work available on the docks. It was a good music town, too. Clubs like the Jazz Workshop in North Beach helped build the cool sounds associated with West Coast Jazz. And bluesmen like Jesse Fuller played the streets. But as the years passed, the longshoremen's jobs dried up or went to Oakland, and rock and roll turned the blues into a venerable ancestor. Of course there were the white imitators during the sixties, and a lot of them were good. Paul Butterfield played here in San Francisco and Mike Bloomfield left Chicago to live and die here. But during those years, the blues was only a branch of the rock revolution.

And yet people told me there was still a lot of music here. They said I should get in touch with Tom Mazzolini, who ran the San Francisco blues festival. He could set me straight, they said. I gave him a call and we agreed to meet at a café on Twenty-fourth Street between Sanchez and Noe. Surely, I figured, he could lead me to the blues.

I got to the café first. Maybe years ago it had been a good bar, but now it specialized in sandwiches with grass on them, imported beer, and overpriced club soda in pretty bottles with exotic labels. I ordered a Miller's and sat at a table on a patio out back. While I waited for Mazzolini, I listened to tasteful murmurings about real estate and stock prices coming from other tables. I lit a cigar. Patrons reeled as if I had committed chemical warfare.

A half hour later, Mazzolini arrived. He was wearing a three-piece suit and carrying a leather attaché case—a camouflaged bluesman. He ordered a bottle of French club soda and frowned at my cigar.

Mazzolini said the blues was still alive in San Francisco and to prove it, he showed me posters from festivals he'd promoted. Most of the acts came from Chicago. Of course he was quick to point out that John Lee Hooker had moved to San Francisco and lived in splendor after years in Detroit poverty. But when he talked about homegrown blues, all he could do was mention a bunch of old men clinging to days gone by.

I sighed. Did the San Francisco blues exist only in the minds of people who lived on Social Security? Apparently, all the affluence had driven the music across the bay to Oakland. Since you could drive out of town for free, I decided to take advantage of the bargain. I drove over to Oakland to see Jimmy McCracklin. My directions led me into the middle of Oakland's ghetto. But, as in Watts, the weather disguised the poverty. McCracklin was staying at the home of his agent, a small shotgun house on Garfield. I was told it would be the house with the Cadillac out front, but when I turned onto Garfield, almost every other house had a Cadillac in the driveway. The McCracklin Cadillac had the biggest rust spots.

Before he became a blues singer, McCracklin was a prize-fighter, so I was cautious with my questions. McCracklin was cautious, too, fumbling with the safety pin that held his shirt together, and eyeing me suspiciously. At first we talked about his career as a prize-fighter. He fought twenty-three bouts before he quit.

"I fought all over the country," he said, easing back into his overstuffed chair. Some of the suspicion drained from his eyes. "I did very good. I won the All-American Light-Heavyweight Championship and then did a lot of fighting while I was in the service. See, I left my home in Helena, Arkansas, when I was nine years old. I used to listen to them blues, man. Sonny Boy Williamson and all them fellas and Walter Davis and all them type of guys. You know, back then, there wasn't nothin' else for you to listen to. Then I left and went to St. Louis. When I first got there, I started going around to the gym and watching Archie Moore and guys like that. I started out at a gym named Slaughter's A.C. That's where I won the St. Louis Golden Gloves.

"After a while, I left St. Louis and goes to Indianapolis. I had quite a few fights down there. And when the war broke out, that's where I joined the Navy. Back in St. Louis, Archie Moore told me if I was ever in California to look him up. And that's where I was stationed, in California.

"But when I got out of the service, I was in this big car wreck. The other guy in the car with me, he died. We were both in the front seat and the steering wheel broke and just knocked me out completely. I got my shoulder hurt and the doctor advised me not to fight no more. So

I said to hell with that game. But this here music, it's the best game. You can stay in this till you're a hundred. Fighting, you're limited in that."

Music may be unlimited, but it's not always lucky. And for Jimmy McCracklin, luck's been hard to find.

"There ain't no dead blues. The blues are big right along. People that was raised up on the blues will always love the music. Just like people who come up on the Jackson Five will always love the Jackson Five. But these big record labels—man, they got to the place now that if you stick your head in the door with the blues, they kick you right out. It's the payola stuff.

"You know, I wrote the biggest song B. B. King ever had. 'The Thrill Is Gone,' I wrote that. I'm a hell of a good writer. I never recorded it. I had a contract with Liberty Records and they had this guy who got all wrapped up trying to manage and produce Bobby Womack. So people like me, we just got dropped along the way. So when I write songs he just say, 'Oh, no, that won't fit you.' They was crooked as a damn snake. They tricked all us writers. But, hell, you pays your dues and you learn.

"'Course after that, I went with Stax in Memphis. You remember that record label? Stax? They went out of business three months after I went with them. They recorded me and three months later they were dead. I keep tellin' you the blues ain't never left, but you take these big R and B radio stations and they've found out they can sell more records to the youth than they can to the old. So they don't play the blues. This is what's happened.

"There's more interest in the blues among the younger set of white folks than among the younger set of black. That's what it's all about. The older set of white folks, once upon a time they wouldn't even listen to our music. They call it junk. It's the young white people that brings it out to the front of the page. But, now, listen here. The average youngster, if he's white, they don't feel these things like we do. What they do, they get a record and then they go to the piano and sit there day after day until they got it down, note by note. They learn how to play the blues, the white kids do, but this was born with us. We've been in the middle of poverty most of our lives and we had to struggle. We had to accept life for what it was. We've always been the underdog in the United States.

"When you really put it together, the blues for us was a way of life. It would give us consolation and them kind of things. The average white kid you see clowning with a guitar, he copies that. It ain't that he feels it, because he probably never had to live the way we did. Oh, there are some poor whites, but how many times have you seen a poor white kid out there struggling to play the blues? Naw, it's the upper-bracket white who is the one who picks up on our stuff. And some of 'em is millionaires. They take our songs, perform 'em before a white audience, and the white kids have a fit. Now, the black guy who recorded it, who writes them things, who put it together from his heart, he don't get no credit for it.

"I don't knock em. I don't care. More power to 'em. What really aggravates me is this: Out of all the stuff I've wrote and recorded—The Beatles did my song 'The Walk' and it was a million-seller, and several other people have cut up my stuff and got rich behind it—I'm still struggling.

"If you ever look at the black acts out there, nine out of ten of them is poor. It's only about one out of fifty that breaks through and he probably didn't get his money. Look at all the people who have recorded songs by people like me and Lowell Folsom and T-Bone Walker. We never got that recognition we wanted or should have had. Those people who do break through, they just over-average lucky. It's not because they the greatest or the best. White people got the money and we don't have it. And this country's run by money. Money is power. And when they use their power against you, it's like fighting a guy with a machine gun and you got a straw.

"If it's ever gonna change, mankind himself's gonna have to change. And that's a problem. A lot of it has to do with plain old black-and-white prejudice. Lots of people these days try to avoid facing facts, but it's there. It's been raised in that older white person that he's superior, that he's better. And he'll die with that inside him. But before he does, he'll teach his feelings to his kids. Say, for instance, you had three daughters. Now what the hell, could you see somebody who looks like me coming up and marrying one of 'em? I mean, in all honesty, I'm giving you the facts. There's something inside of you that says, 'Hell, I don't want nothing black marrying my daughter.' And I'd have to feel the same way if I had a daughter and she wanted to marry a white boy. Because that's been raised up in me. I just feel like the qualifications ain't for them to be together. It's not that he ain't as good as I am or I ain't as good as he is—that ain't the problem. It's just the idea of color, and that will be forever in peoples. You can take that right back to music. There's a lot of white kids playing before an audience today who can't even carry a tune good. But as far as white audiences are concerned, they're better than a Jimmy McCracklin."

He sighed, seemed to shake off some of the bitterness. Then he talked for a while about a new album he was making. It would be a hit. He was sure of it. And, in fact, with a new manager and a new awareness, he still had a chance. He'd paid his dues. Now it was his turn. Maybe even some of his old songs could sell again.

"You know," he said, "a record is just like people. It lives and dies. The only differences in records and peoples is that people don't come back. Records can."

McCracklin had calmed down and wanted to play me some cuts from an album he had just recorded. Sure, I said, I'll listen. But it was apparent our discussion was over.

I left Oakland and drove south along the bay, past Berkeley and over to El Cerrito to see Chris Strachwitz. In the 1950s he had traveled throughout Texas and Mississippi recording blues singers for his new Arhoolie label. He was also the first person to record Louisiana zydeco music, the first to make Clifton Chenier famous. The world of the blues he helped discover was gone now, but I figured he could reconstruct it for me.

Strachwitz was born in Germany, came to this country when he was a child, and developed an immediate love for American music. In the late 1960s, he recorded "Feel Like I'm Fixin' to Die Rag" for Country Joe and the Fish. The band didn't have any money, so Strachwitz agreed to make the record for the publishing rights to the song. Nobody knew it would become the quintessential anti-Vietnam protest song. When it did, Strachwitz got enough money to build a new headquarters for his Arhoolie Records and Down Home Music record store.

I pulled into the parking lot on San Pablo Avenue and went inside. Strachwitz was waiting for me. He was wearing a pastel cable-knit sweater and looked California-healthy. When he spoke there was just a hint of a German accent. But Strachwitz, as I soon found out, is a talented mimic and at times, the accent vanished as he imitated the voices of the blues men he once recorded. He was hungry and wanted to eat at the Chinese restaurant across the street.

"It's not bad," he said, "if you tell them not to bring gravy."

"Sure," I said, "no gravy's fine with me." I was beginning to understand the bay area. No cigars, no gravy, and not much bourbon.

Over lunch, he talked about his love for music and his days on the road, looking for the ultimate unknown blues singer.

"I think I've always been sort of fascinated by records," he said as we waited for the fish he'd ordered. "My mother, back in the early thirties, brought me back some seventy-eights when I was a kid. And I remember I played those things on the windup. I just loved the discs. I remember one of them was Al Jolson's 'Sonny Boy.' And some other American things. You know, there was just a kind of beat on those records I didn't hear in Germany.

"After the war, I really fell in love with music I heard on the Armed Forces Network. So when I came here, I was totally addicted to the radio. Especially when they sent me to school in Southern California. That's where I first heard gospel music. It was a church choir on KFVD on Sunday night. Then there was the Harlem Matinee with Hunter Hancock. It was an early rhythm-and-blues show. Oh, yeah. That's also the time I fell in love with XERB, a big powerful station in Rosarito Beach in Baja, California. They'd play these fifteen-minute programs devoted to the Maddox Brothers and Rose or Roy Acuff or the Armstrong Twins.

"Now, the first blues I ever heard, I think it was sort of a culmination of things. Of course, I was always interested in New Orleans music, ever since a friend in high school took me to see a movie called *New Orleans*. So I went out and bought everything. There was a Bunk Johnson four-disc album and I bought a couple of Kid Ory records. So I was a real New Orleans jazz freak.

"Then I heard Lightnin' Hopkins on the radio. I think it was in Reno and it must have been in 1952 or 1951. I had a grandmother in Reno and she had a gardener who knew I was crazy about this kind of music. Now, there was a joint called the Harlem Club, a black club, down by the railroad station. And I went there. Saw a piano player there and I asked him where he was from. He said Oakland. I have no idea who he was but he sounded like Big Maceo. Low-down blues, is what it was.

"I used to hear Jesse Fuller. I remember I heard him at the Tin Angel. He was the first one I ever taped, actually. Then I decided I wanted to make records. I bought old records for cheap and I sold them overseas for a little bit more and made my first money to buy a tape recorder. It was a very romantic thing.

"I went in the Army and got discharged in 1955. They discharged me in 1956 at Fort Chaffee, Arkansas. And that was so close to New Orleans that I had to go there. New Orleans was still my first love. There I saw Billie and Dede Pierce and George Lewis's band at the Paddock Club."

The fish came and Strachwitz cut it in half and served it, careful not to touch a drop of the little bit of gravy left on the plate.

"Later, I met Sam Charters, the blues historian. I met him up here and when we talked he went on and on about those Southern trips he had taken before. I think secretly I must have been idolizing him. He could go on a trip and come home with a bunch of those beat-up old records of things I'd never seen, like a Memphis jug band. Then I remember he got interested in Lightnin' Hopkins. He used to come over and listen to my records by him.

"Then all of a sudden, I got a postcard from Houston, Texas, saying, 'I found Lightnin' Hopkins.' None of us had the sense to call up the record labels and ask where this man comes from. It was a romantic thing. I remember the French jazz magazine *Jazz Hot* had articles about Lightnin' Hopkins and they said they had no idea where he was from. He was a Mississippi native but he sounded more like Texas. But nobody really knew where he was. Then we found out.

"Later, my sister needed a car driven to Alburquerque, New Mexico. I said, 'Why that can't be too far from Houston.' Ha! It was a long bus ride from New Mexico to East Texas.

"In Houston, I stayed at the YMCA. That's when I met Lightnin' Hopkins, and that's when I decided I really wanted a record company. I recorded him, but I never really got him the way I wanted it. I had never heard anything in my life like Lightnin' Hopkins in those beer joints. There would be hardly anybody there but he would be playing and making up these songs.

"The best thing I can remember is when I walked in a joint and he was playing this real low-down blues. Then he'd sing, 'Oh, man, this man come all the way from California just to hear po' Lightnin' Sing.' I remember that was one of the verses and I just couldn't believe it. I can't remember all the rhymes, but he sang about almost not being able to make it to work that night because it had rained so hard and the rain covered all the chuck holes. He rhymed it all up. He was singing about how his shoulder was aching because his arthritis was acting up.

"It's like if you had somebody telling you stories. But there was constantly this bashing drum behind him. Pounding away. It was the most haunting thing I'd seen. And I was fascinated by the whole culture.

"Then I hung out with Lightnin' one night. He said, 'Man, I want to do some gambling. Come on, I'll show you how to play some dominoes.' So we knocked on the door of this dark house. I said, 'There's nobody here.' And Lightnin' says, 'Yeah, he's in there,' and he kept pounding on the door. Finally, this sleepy black guy comes out and says, 'Hey, what you want?' Lightnin' says, 'I want to play some dominoes.' The guy says, 'Come on in.' He figured Lightnin' would have some money. They both sat down at a table and I started watching the roaches running around the room. I'd never seen creatures like that," Strachwitz said. "They were walking over the planks and they were huge. Lightnin' was pretty alert. And the other guy, I thought he was asleep. But they'd throw the dice and as soon as those dice settled, that other guy knew what the numbers were.

"Another time we went to the sanctified church. Sometimes there would be two drummers bashing away. You know, *dum-dum-dum-Jesus-dum-dum-dum*. I made a film later, in 1961, and we caught some of that. They made me get on the altar. They said, 'We got to have some lights,' and they were just rocking. It was unbelievable.

"The same year that I met Lightnin', I had an inkling that in Washington County, Texas, a man named Tom Moore might be there. Lightnin' had made a song in the 1940s about Tom Moore. Some of those lines were, 'There ain't but one thing this man's done wrong. Leave his wife and baby on Mr. Tom Moore's farm.' It has lines like, 'You go see Mr. Moore for five, he'll haul off and give you ten.'

That is, you'll ask him for five dollars and he'll actually loan you ten just to keep you further in debt. Then the song says, 'Then come Christmastime, your woman runs off and leaves you, you just talk to Mr. Moore and he'll bring her back.' I thought it was just an imaginary thing. But then I decided to go out into the blues country.

"So we drove out into Washington County, northwest of Houston. We'd see people working in the fields, working with hoes and stuff. And we'd say, 'You guys know any good guitar players?' They'd say, 'Go to Navasota.' So we went to the feed store. So I asked, 'Does Mr. Tom Moore live in this town?' And I found out he had an office on top of the bank building. I went to his office and asked if he had somebody who played for suppers, one of his hired hands. He said, 'There's a guy, but I don't know his name, but you can ask Peg Leg down at the railroad station. I don't know his name either, but you can't miss him. He's only got one leg.'

"So we went to the railroad station and we asked Peg Leg about the guitar player. He said the man's name was Mance Lipscomb. Well, we showed up at Mance's house that night and I recorded him. I liked him as a man, but I didn't like his music. He was too sweet, almost. He wasn't a nasty blues singer like Lightnin' was. He sang all these funny little songs. But I figured this was the oldest stuff I was gonna find and that Alan Lomax at the Library of Congress would give his right foot for this. So that's what the first record was.

"On that same trip I recorded Black Ace in Fort Worth. I found him on a street corner. I mean, you go into these black neighborhoods and they were just playing dice on the street. I asked if they knew a guy named Little Brother, and they all looked at me and asked, 'What you want with him?' And I said, 'I like his records and want to record him.'

'Yeah,' they said, 'he hangs out with Black Ace. Every night at five he comes to this bar and you can't miss him. He'll have a white shirt on and it'll say ACE on his shirt.' So, sure enough, I went there at five o'clock and a man came up to me wearing a white shirt that said ACE on it. He hadn't played for a while, but we got him cranked up and got him some new strings. He still had his old guitar, a big Hawaiian National guitar that he played on his lap."

Strachwitz swallowed his last bite of fish and patted his lips with a napkin.

"But that was then. More than thirty years ago. This is now. I haven't done too much hunting around, but I don't think there is much anymore."

I thought about what Strachwitz said as I paid the toll and drove back to San Francisco. He was right. The days of discovering the unknown blues singer on southern back roads was over. It ended, ironically, because black Americans gained the right to be complete citizens.

And as they gained voting rights and the right to sit anywhere they wanted at restaurants and movie theaters, the right to sleep in any hotel room and, supposedly, live in any subdivision, they became acculturated by consumerism. Black culture—and the blues is the root of it—flourished in its separateness. Because blacks were not allowed to be part of white America, they formed their own country hidden beneath the Jim Crow line. Whites stole from them frequently. Otherwise there would have been no Original Dixieland Jass Band, no Swing and Sway with Sammy Kay, no Lindy Hop, no Charleston, no Rock and

Roll. Black influence is what made the distinctive American culture.

But the blues was always there—separate and distinct—acting as a venerable grandmother, keeping the new ways close to the ground, making sure that history was not forgotten. Acculturation ended all that. Middle-class black families, not wanting to be reminded of the struggle of their people only a generation ago, prefer the more cerebral music of Charlie Parker and the Modern Jazz Quartet. And in the ghettos, the kids listen to disco because it's what most black radio stations play. Whitney Houston is only black because her skin is dark, not because of any cultural difference that radiates from her music. More than ever, the route to success in America has become the white road. And blacks with ambition realize they must adopt that culture as their own to get ahead. Prosperity in America often means white bread and mayonnaise. But acculturation has not meant the end of racism. It is no longer as overt, but by refusing to accept black culture unless it's been run though a Caucasian filter, it's just as insidious. Add to that the conglomeratization of the record business—there are only five major labels left in the United States and two of them are foreign-owned—and you can see why the blues is forced to struggle.

The irony of that, of course, is that it's white people who are keeping the blues alive. Around the country there are blues societies in every city, functioning in the same way chamber-music clubs do. Neither form has much popular appeal anymore, but the faithful make sure the music lives, at least on some sort of life-support system. Just as there is a Chamber Music Festival in Santa Fe, there are blues festivals in Baton Rouge, Chicago, Washington,

Memphis, Chattanooga, the Mississippi Delta, and Ann Arbor, Michigan. And it's mostly white people who attend.

Years ago, my family refused to allow hillbilly music to be played at home. We were a generation removed from the backwater sounds of Hank Williams and Ernest Tubb and to prove it we listened to Mantovani and the Ray Coniff Singers. No one was going to call us hillbillies, and if they did, they'd have a hard time proving it. That, I suspect, is why there are discos on the Delta where there used to be juke joints, why Bill Cosby as a prosperous middle-class doctor is the role model for blacks, why the emotion of the blues has been sublimated.

There are places on The Blues Route where the blues still flourish, cities where looking for a blues joint is not like a quest for the Holy Grail. In Chicago the blues is strong with younger musicians choosing that as their preferred way of expression. And in Louisiana, particularly in the Cajun regions, zydeco is alive with no preservation needed.

Most people say the blues will never die. They're right. Jazz musicians still rely on the blues for most of their compositions; rock-and-roll performers must pay homage to it. But like any ancestor, it has become an influence, not the driving force it once was.

Yet the patient has amazing strength. Just when the obit is written, the coffin bought, the flowers ordered, there is a resurgence. I thought about that as I packed my bags and headed to the airport. I was going home. On the radio I heard Whitney Houston. I reached over and snapped it off, preferring instead to hear in my mind the words of Magic Slim at the Checkerboard Lounge in Chicago when he sang:

"Hey, hey! The blues is all right!"